D1548050

Fifty Years
of Segregation

Fifty Years
of Segregation

Black Higher Education
in Kentucky, 1904-1954

John A. Hardin

The University Press of Kentucky

Publication of this volume was made possible in part
by a grant from the National Endowment for the Humanities.

Scholarly publisher for the Commonwealth,
serving Bellarmine College, Berea College, Centre
College of Kentucky, Eastern Kentucky University,
The Filson Club Historical Society, Georgetown College,
Kentucky Historical Society, Kentucky State University,
Morehead State University, Murray State University,
Northern Kentucky University, Transylvania University,
University of Kentucky, University of Louisville,
and Western Kentucky University.

Editorial and Sales Offices: The University Press of Kentucky
663 South Limestone Street, Lexington, Kentucky 40508-4008

01 00 99 98 97 5 4 3 2 1

Library of Congress Cataloging-in-Publication Data

Hardin, John A., 1948-
    Fifty years of segregation : black higher education in Kentucky,
    1904-1954 / John A. Hardin.
        p. cm.
    Includes bibliographical references and index.
    ISBN 0-8131-2024-1 (alk. paper)
    1. Segregation in higher education—Kentucky—History. 2. Afro-
American universities and colleges—Kentucky—History. I. Title.
LC212.722.K4H37   1997
378.769'08996073—dc21   97-18586

This book is printed on acid-free recycled paper meeting
the requirements of the American National Standard
for Permanence in Paper for Printed Library Materials.

Manufactured in the United States of America

Contents

Illustrations follow page 88.

Preface

KENTUCKY'S BLACK COLLEGES have produced several generations of teachers, public servants, businessmen, and community leaders in an era when racial segregation was the norm and black expectations for success were limited at best, yet the story of these institutions has received little attention from scholars. In 1972, after passage of the 1960s legislation ending de jure segregation, I began my teaching career at Kentucky State University. There, I discovered that Kentucky blacks had struggled since 1904 to craft strategies that would end segregated education at all levels. From my initial peek into Kentucky's past has evolved a doctoral dissertation, several scholarly articles, and a popular history of Kentucky State University. I hope this work will not be the last to examine the ways twentieth-century Kentucky blacks overcame the disabilities of racial caste.

This humble effort reflects the wise counsel and support of many colleagues and associates. Among them are Henry E. Cheaney, Terry Birdwhistell, Felix Boateng, Lowell Harrison, James Klotter, Mary Langford, Richard Langford, Gerald Linderman, Marion Lucas, and Gerald Smith. Archival staff at the following were gracious in providing assistance and research data: Berea College, Eastern Kentucky University, Eastern Washington University, the Filson Club Historical Society, University of Kentucky, the Kentucky Historical Society, Kentucky State University, University of Louisville, Murray State University, and Western Kentucky University. A special thanks to Western Kentucky University Faculty Research Committee for its financial support and the Department of History for the time to work on the project.

Introduction

AS THE SMOKE of the Civil War battles cleared in 1865, Americans, in particular those of African descent, lived for the first time in a national culture without chattel slavery. The immediate concern for blacks was survival as emancipated men and women in a society where they did not enjoy the full rights, privileges, and immunities of citizenship. Aware of this conundrum, thoughtful blacks equipped themselves for their predicament by pursuing what they could not easily obtain before emancipation: an education. Organizations and individuals previously involved in the fight for abolition of American slavery now focused their efforts on the education of freed blacks. The American Missionary Association, the Slater Fund, the Anna T. Jeanes Fund and, much later, the General Education Board committed extensive resources to black education over a period that extended well into the twentieth century. At the same time, these organizations supported the existing social order, in which blacks remained subordinate to southern whites, who would be allowed to restart the region's economy and reconstruct their state governments.

At Virginia's Hampton Institute and later at Tuskegee Institute in Alabama, presidents Samuel C. Armstrong and Booker T. Washington argued that blacks would best contribute to this process via industrial education, an approach that limited blacks to agriculture and semi-skilled occupations not wanted by white workers. In this scheme of the future, industrial education became the key process to transform formerly enslaved blacks into subordinate employees, with white local authorities and worker supervisors maintaining paramount control and reaping the benefits.[1]

Not all white southerners were supportive of efforts to educate blacks for citizenship. Most northern campaigns to educate blacks in the 1860s and 1870s were directed toward the former Confederate and slaveholding states where there had been large black populations and where their formal education had been ignored. One of these states, Kentucky, occupied a unique position before, during, and after the war. Kentucky supported slavery but did not join the Confederacy. When the war ended, the state legislature refused to ratify the Thirteenth Amendment and incredulously aligned itself with southern states by refusing to spend public money to educate its black citizens and by enacting racial segregation statutes. All the while, Kentucky blacks preserved and used their right to vote in spite of violent intimidation by white terrorist groups. Given this racist treatment, Kentucky blacks persisted in their demands for equal treatment under the law by local and state authorities.

As white-controlled legislatures began spending more public funds on education in the 1860s, Kentucky blacks fought for their fair share despite the legal roadblocks. Under an 1866 state constitutional amendment, blacks and whites could not be taught together.[2] Taxes collected from blacks and whites were spent on white common schools, and if there were enough funds left over, black schools received support. When the prospect of litigation forced the state legislature in 1882 to equalize public school appropriations, Kentucky school officials began seriously to support black public schools.[3]

Although meager initially, state support for these schools expanded black community interest in organizing and supporting local educational institutions. Under postbellum state laws, blacks paid property taxes that funded schools but excluded blacks from enrollment. Blacks paid additional taxes or contributed in-kind materials, for example, lumber, to establish racially segregated public schools. Deep South blacks during the Reconstruction era accepted that condition as a part of the sanctioned social order. However, some Kentucky blacks, who operated private schools in Louisville as early as 1847, were determined to reestablish their schools and to resume educating their children after the war's end.[4]

Teachers for these schools were the greatest need in 1865. (Facilities at early stages were less important because black churches often doubled as classrooms.) White missionary teachers gradually focused their energies on other states with larger black populations. This change made attracting teachers from normal schools more critical. Kentucky blacks struggled on their own to hire qualified "race" (or black) teachers when "Yankee schoolmarms" went elsewhere. Kentucky whites almost universally abdicated their responsibility, saying the "Yankees freed them, now let the Yankees take care of them."[5]

The first important organized group that supported a normal school came from the Kentucky General Association of Colored Baptists, established in 1865 as an organization for the commonwealth's black Baptists. This body, representing the largest black religious group in the state, served as a locus for discussion of the issue. Its interest in establishing such a school centered on the desire of black Baptists to create a ministerial teacher training facility under denominational control.

The campaign to create a state-supported teacher training school persisted among black educators and organizations but failed to make any substantive headway in the conservative, white-controlled legislature. In 1877, after agitation by the Kentucky Colored State Teachers Association and church groups, Superintendent of Public Instruction Howard A.M. Henderson convened a meeting of the state's black school teachers to discuss the issue. The meeting reinvigorated the black Baptist association's sporadic efforts to establish a school of its own that would include normal as well as theological curricula.[6] After these meetings and upon securing financial support from the state's white Baptists, the association opened the Kentucky Normal and Theological Institute in 1879 at a Louisville site.[7]

The school's religious mission initially excluded industrial courses favored by contemporary white philanthropic organizations and black leaders such as Booker T. Washington. Kentucky's black Baptists wanted a school primarily to train future ministers as well as other students who wanted a liberal arts education. By 1884 the institute trustees had changed its name to State Colored Baptist University to reflect its denominational connection and the right of each state senator to send one "properly equipped student" from his district at state expense.[8] With the addition of college courses to its elementary and secondary level programs, State University became Kentucky's first black-owned, comprehensive educational institution. Within the next decade several local black, private professional schools that were faced with financial shortfalls merged with State University: Harper Law School, Louisville National Medical College, and Central Law School. These additions spurred such confidence in State University that white adjunct faculty members were added to the medical college faculty. By 1900 State University in Louisville had become the central location for black higher education in Kentucky.

The growth of State University sprang from its leadership. After its first year (1879-80) under founder Elijah P. Marrs, the trustees appointed William J. Simmons to head the school. Although he professed public support for the Hampton-Tuskegee educational model, Simmons still supported black schools with either all-industrial education programs or all-liberal arts curricula; at that time he considered hybrid institutions with both types of programs unacceptable.

Simmons's tenure at State University ended abruptly in early 1890, when he resigned the presidency to establish Eckstein Norton Institute at Cane Spring, Kentucky. Named after Louisville and Nashville Railroad executive and patron Eckstein Norton, the institution followed a mostly industrial education path rather than the diverse curricular approach of State University. Operating with this narrow focus, the institute struggled for survival after Simmons's sudden death in October 1890. Although managed effectively by Simmons's protégé Charles Henry Parrish, dwindling enrollments and shrinking resources led to the school's eventual merger with Lincoln Institute in Simpsonville, Kentucky.[9]

In contrast to the private support given State University and Eckstein Norton Institute, the publicly supported Kentucky State Normal School for Colored Persons (which I will refer to as Kentucky State) was established in 1886 with limited resources and sparse attendance. After a brisk competition among seven Kentucky cities for the school, a donation of land from the Frankfort city council confirmed its site. The state legislature made initial biennial commitments of three thousand dollars for operating expenses and seven thousand dollars for classroom construction. In its first term Kentucky State had three teachers, fifty-five students, one building, and an industrial teacher training curriculum.[10]

Gradually, the school attracted more students during its first decade and took advantage of provisions of the 1890 Morrill Land Grant Act to acquire additional moneys and property. With them the school received increasing amounts of political and economic support from Kentucky whites who advocated the Hampton-Tuskegee industrial education philosophy. In his report to the white trustees later forwarded to the state school board, school president John Henry Jackson, mindful of the white acceptance of the Hampton-Tuskegee paradigm, praised the trustees for their support of the school's industrial education efforts "by encouraging and promoting, by every means in [their] power, those industrial pursuits that are so wholesome and so helpful in raising up a class of producers." Jackson, who had received a classical college education at Kentucky's integrated Berea College, had no alternative but to praise the industrial education paradigm. To justify his requests for increased funding for new facilities for mechanical courses, he argued that the school produced "skilled mechanics, scientific agriculturalists and females trained in domestic economy." The presence of workers with such skills, he maintained, improved both the "moral and intellectual well-being" of each community.[11]

Jackson, while praising the soundness of industrial education for blacks, neglected to mention what everyone knew implicitly, that this philosophy encouraged black subordination to white employers. Rather than depriving whites of employment, as some whites had feared, occupations in agriculture and domestic service were designated informally as respectable "negro jobs" after proper training in an industrial education normal school such as Kentucky State.[12]

As this movement for diverting blacks into industrial education attracted increasing support both nationally and regionally, the state legislature recognized its potential usefulness as trainers of workers for the commonwealth's agriculture, coal, light manufacturing, and thoroughbred horse industries. To make the industrial education approach feasible, the legislature provided additional land and facilities for Kentucky State through special laws in 1893, 1896, and 1897.[13] Given this additional support for less-than-collegiate–level industrial education, Kentucky State served at least two purposes. In its early years it enabled the state to remove black teacher training from the outside influence of northern whites at Berea College, and it diluted the influence of the state's black Baptists on higher education.

At the turn of the century, three issues clouded the future of higher education for Kentucky blacks: the funding of black secondary education, the movement for accommodation to segregation by black leaders, and the decline of white liberal support at such places as Berea College.

Confronted by white indifference toward black activist attacks on segregation laws, Kentucky blacks continued their private financial contributions to the inadequately funded public, all-black high schools in Covington, Frankfort, Lexington, Louisville, Owensboro, Paducah, Paris, and Winchester.[14] One faction of black educators, however, received measured white acceptance. After a widely celebrated 1895 Atlanta speech by Booker T. Washington of Alabama's Tuskegee Institute, favoring both southern white control and industrial education, Washington's ideological supporters at Kentucky State and Eckstein Norton Institute enjoyed increased financial support from the white power structure.

In spite of Washington's accommodation to dominant southern white views on race, one Kentucky college refused to enforce rigid racial segregation. Since 1866 many Kentucky blacks had attended the jewel of racially integrated southern colleges, Berea College, which required its students, regardless of race, to undergo both industrial training and classical education. However, hostility toward black participation at Berea College had begun to increase in the 1890s from without and within. Appalachian white students and unsympathetic Berea College administrators had lost the fervor for interracial education advocated in 1866 by its abolitionist founder, John Gregg Fee. In moving away from Fee's original vision, the college's administrators, like many whites in other areas of life, enforced and hardened a color line that W.E.B. Du Bois predicted would be the major social problem of the twentieth century.

Although the color line started to take shape as the Civil War ended, its dominant presence in Kentucky communities took longer to create. In a border state later described by jurist Thurgood Marshall as "civil" toward black litigants, educated Kentucky blacks fought in the courts to hold on to liberties guaranteed by the Fourteenth and Fifteenth Amendments. The activism of educated Kentucky blacks, carried out in their own special ways, affected the social fiber of the state more than the small numbers of blacks would suggest. This narrative on Kentucky black higher education does not focus, therefore, on curricula or educational philosophies per se but on a half-century of internal struggles and institutional adaptations by educated blacks who emerged from a complex labyrinth of antebellum racial prejudice. Their largely untold story exposes both black capitulations to racism and small triumphs by other blacks over travails associated with racially segregated higher education.

On the surface, this account appears no different from that of other southern states. But Kentucky was not geographically in the Deep South. The social history of the post–Civil War Deep South included a canon of racial segregation traditions that required the social separation of blacks and whites from womb to tomb. Kentucky, with a smaller black population, often deviated from the accepted racial practices. Unlike those in other southern states, Kentucky blacks voted unhampered and were politically active in urban areas. They were elected to local offices in counties with large black populations. These isolated deviations permitted the state to practice what historian George C. Wright described as "genteel" or polite racism.

This study concerns Kentucky's efforts to impose an important part of that polite racism—racially segregated public and private higher education—on educated, twentieth-century blacks who, for their own complex and tactical reasons, initially tolerated it but soon rebelled and ultimately rejected it. Kentucky civil rights activists subsequently used these experiences in fighting segregated education in their attack on other forms of racial discrimination in the 1950s. They started to disestablish them, and other activists continued the task in the 1960s. Black educators in Kentucky, as well as those few whites who recognized the basic unfairness of racial segregation, fought for equality of higher education for blacks to prove that truly equal educational opportunities could exist. Largely ignored by most civil rights historians, these Kentucky battles for higher education equity from 1904 to 1954 served both as early, critical skirmishes in the national struggles for de jure civil rights and as test sites for activist strategies. For these reasons, the story of Kentucky's agonizing experience with segregated black higher education must be told.

To explain how Kentucky educators operated their system of higher education circumscribed by a color line, this study identifies the state's leading black educators from 1904 to 1954 and compares their ideologies of education for blacks and the quiet, often unseen struggles to implement them. It also examines the gradual evolution of the institutions that these educators administered and the internal conflicts among them in this period and thereafter. The saga begins in 1904 when a newly enacted Kentucky law forced Berea College, one of the South's few integrated, private colleges in the early twentieth century, to exclude its 174 black students because of their race. As opposition to the segregation law faded, such administrators at black institutions as Green Pinckney Russell and Dennis H. Anderson grudgingly accepted the political correctness of racially segregated higher education. Within this social order, two factions developed among Kentucky black educators. In the years following 1904, the majority supported Washington's Hampton-Tuskegee model of industrial education, while a minority supported classical, liberal arts curricula for Kentucky's black collegians. When industrial education gradually lost its popularity in the late 1920s, black awareness of the social weakness of industrial education led to its rejection as the paramount educational philosophy for blacks.

During this era that paralleled the Depression, national and regional toleration of segregation by blacks began to change. Civil rights activists within the education profession disputed the prevailing white belief that segregated education, higher or otherwise, was somehow positive for blacks. By 1930, moreover, the industrial education philosophy in the state's segregated black colleges had come under fire from most black educators. Black state representative and civil rights activist Charles W. Anderson Jr. also challenged the state's alleged "equal" educational opportunities for blacks as being unequal. By 1930, the liberal arts-based teacher education curricula at Kentucky State and Louisville Municipal College gradually replaced the older, narrowly focused industrial education programs.

As the turmoil of World War Two ended, American blacks who had fought to end Nazi fascism overseas became dissatisfied with a de jure second-class citizenship enforced under state statutes. Lawsuits by blacks against segregation policies proliferated as victory over Hitlerian terror was celebrated and the campaign to fight international communism developed. Without financial aid from the national attorneys of the NAACP, Kentucky blacks financed their own anti–school segregation litigation in 1948. The national NAACP gave special attention to five lawsuits concerning public school segregation in other states. These cases, in concert with legal challenges filed by Kentucky civil rights activists, led to significant reversals of state law controlling segregated schools and colleges.

As the landmark 1954 *Brown v. Board of Education* rulings disrupted the national legal foundations of racial segregation, Kentucky continued to make progress toward the destruction of segregated education at all levels. The peaceful desegregation of Kentucky's colleges and schools constituted a benchmark in the 1950s and 1960s for other states to follow. In the 1970s, however, violent white resistance in Louisville to busing to achieve school desegregation demonstrated that the black struggle for equal educational opportunities had not ended. In the 1980s Kentucky was ordered by the federal government to end vestiges of segregation in higher education, a condition that some thought was long gone. These events again reminded the nation and, more precisely, Kentuckians, that the color line, once created, had become a difficult and perplexing social institution to disestablish.

1

Hardening the Color Line, 1904-1910

THE TWENTIETH-CENTURY racial color line predicted by W.E.B. Du Bois materialized differently across the nation. From 1904 to 1910, Kentucky whites hardened racial barriers created after the Civil War. Kentucky whites also rationalized racial segregation as a moderate, morally sound policy to keep the peace. Although it was not a centrally managed campaign, Kentucky politicians recognized the need to control both poor whites who received substandard education and blacks who were insistent on fair treatment. In this context black and white educators were forced to accept legislative and political mandates to implement racial segregation in public and private schools and, if necessary, create new all-black ones to fulfill the mandate.

The legal foundation originated in 1866 when the Kentucky legislature passed an amendment to the state constitution that required racially segregated public schools. By 1904 one site of interracial education remained in the state's private schools. To correct the omission, the 1904 Kentucky legislature imitated other southern and border states and extended the existing prohibition of racially integrated education to private schools. This law followed one state legislator's outrage about the racially integrated, private Berea College, in Berea, Kentucky.

Kentucky blacks who lived in the state's mountainous, eastern coal-producing region attended Berea College, a racially integrated, private institution affiliated with the American Missionary Association since its founding in 1866 by abolitionist John Gregg Fee. At Berea, blacks completed their secondary education, trained in an "industry," and received an education leading to a bachelor's degree. Unlike other Kentucky schools that called them-selves col-leges, Berea College received financial support from out-of-state philanthropists and was thus able to hire competent out-of-state fac-ulty in the classics and in vocational fields. As a result Berea College graduates were well prepared either to teach or to work in several professions.

From the perspective of early-twentieth-century Kentuckians, Berea represented a unique educational situation. Class offerings in-cluded liberal arts courses in grammar, rhetoric, fine arts, and sci-ences. Before graduation all students fulfilled a college requirement to master an industry in the campus craft shops. Berea's blend of vo-cational and liberal arts education made it attractive to the region's black and white citizens.[1] The college's tradition of interracial educa-tion, introduced by its abolitionist founder, remained popular among blacks because they received the same instruction as their white peers. White Kentuckians tolerated the college's integrated campus because wealthy, out-of-state contributors kept the institution viable without the use of local donations.

Not everyone approved of the college's unique biracial atmos-phere, however. Following the 1895 Atlanta Exposition speech by black educator Booker T. Washington, in which he condoned racial segregation, Berea's interracial practices appeared out of step with current thought on racial relations. Although Berea's President William C. Frost told white audiences that he directed college re-sources toward Appalachian whites, southern whites remained un-convinced.[2] In 1901 neighboring Tennessee passed a law excluding blacks from privately operated Maryville College and forced an end to interracial education at church-owned schools in the state.[3]

In early 1904 Carl Day, a Democratic state legislator from pre-dominantly white, rural Breathitt County, became disturbed about Berea's interracial policy. He apparently witnessed a fair-skinned black female who he thought was white give a friendly kiss to another black female student at the Berea railroad station, and he became incensed at this suggestion of egalitarian conduct between whites and blacks. Encouraged by Berea townsfolk who opposed the college's uncomfortable experiment with interracial education, Day translated his anger into a bill that prohibited private corporations such as Berea College from teaching students of different races in the same room. With public school racial segregation firmly in place, Day's bill proposed to put an end to interracial education in the commonwealth by including private schools such as Berea.[4] Despite impassioned speeches in the legislature by President Frost and several white Berea students opposing the law, the legislature approved Day's bill with only five dissenting votes in the House of Representatives and five in the Senate. The last vestige of biracial education in Kentucky, and in the entire South, had come to an abrupt end.[5]

The passage of the Day Law forced the college trustees to either exclude all black students or violate the law. The trustees took the middle ground and did both. They allowed black students to remain temporarily but encouraged them to attend other "good schools" that accepted them. In the 1904-5 year, 52 of the 174 enrolled blacks transferred—at Berea's expense—to other schools, including Fisk University, Knoxville College, Tuskegee Institute, and Kentucky State. The remaining black students were encouraged to do likewise. The trustees, largely white, non-Kentucky philanthropists, believed this policy satisfied the immediate needs of black Berea students and removed them from any immediate legal penalties.[6] Representative Day and the large majority of the legislature had achieved a practical, moral goal: blacks and whites were to be educated separately in order to preserve white racial sanctity and social order.

Although the college administrators and trustees agreed on the plan to remove its black students, the trustees also resolved to oppose the Day Law through a legal test in the courts based on founder Fee's belief in interracial education. To handle the legal challenge, Berea trustees hired three eminent lawyers: John G. Carlisle, Curtis F. Burnham, and Guy F. Mallon. Carlisle had served as a speaker of the U.S. House of Representatives and as treasury secretary under Pres. Grover Cleveland. Burnham served in the Kentucky Senate and was one of the five senators who voted against the House version of the Day Law. Mallon operated a thriving law practice in Cincinnati.

On 12 October 1904 the Madison County Grand Jury indicted the college on two counts of violating those portions of the Day Law that required blacks and whites to be taught in separate classrooms and instruction to be carried on in buildings no fewer than twenty-five miles apart. Found guilty in Madison Circuit Court of violating both sections of the law, Berea College paid a one-thousand-dollar fine.[7]

Subsequently, Berea's attorneys carried the case to the Kentucky Court of Appeals and argued that the state had abused its police powers and had denied students, teachers, and trustees their rights guaranteed in the bill of rights of the Kentucky constitution and in the Fourteenth Amendment of the U.S. Constitution, which protected the rights of liberty, worship, happiness, free speech, and property ownership.[8]

They further argued that because the twenty-sixth section of the Kentucky Bill of Rights invalidated any law that conflicted with these rights, the Day Law, which abridged Berean rights under the Kentucky constitution, was unconstitutional. The commonwealth's argument, however, rested on an implied duty to maintain public order by enforcing racial segregation. The case brief summarized not only the state's position but also the white conventional wisdom on racial segregation:

> The natural separation of the race[s] is therefore an undeniable fact, and all social organizations which lead to their amalgamation are repugnant to the law of nature. From social amalgamation it is but a step to illicit intercourse, and but another [to] intermarriage. But to assert separateness is not to declare inferiority in either; it is not to declare one a slave and [the] other a freeman—that would be to draw the illogical sequence of inferiority from difference[s] only. . . . It is simply to say that following the order of Divine Providence, human authority ought not to compel these widely separate races to intermix.[9]

As for the legal right of the state to use its regulatory authority on Berea College, the court declared that amalgamation of the races was an evil sufficient to justify the use of state police powers to forbid interracial education.[10] The court nullified the second count against the college because the requirement that a separate black school be at least twenty-five miles away from a white one was deemed oppressive.

The court's ruling supported the state's argument that teaching was not a protected right. Under the constitution, the state exercised its power to regulate a corporation such as Berea College. The state also limited the corporation's authority to teach students in racially mixed classrooms. The court presumed these classes to be harmful to the public welfare.[11]

In an April 1908 appeal in the U.S. Supreme Court, the college attorneys argued that if one part of the law (i.e., section 4, which required separate instruction of races twenty-five miles apart) was unconstitutional, the entire law became unconstitutional. The defendant (the commonwealth) argued that the intent of the law was to use the state's police power to prohibit the voluntary association of whites and blacks by a corporation and nothing more. The invalidation of the one section should not void the entire law. In November 1908 the Court majority agreed with the defendant and ruled against the plaintiff's arguments presented in section 4 because the power of states to regulate corporations—Berea College—had more standing than racial discrimination.[12]

Like the Kentucky Court of Appeals ruling, the vote was not unanimous. Of the three dissenting opinions—Judge John J. Baker of the Kentucky Court of Appeals and Justices John Marshall Harlan and William Day of the Supreme Court—Harlan's became the most compelling.

Harlan, a native Kentuckian and a Republican appointee, dissented on two grounds, insisting first that, if the appeals court voided section 4 of the law, the entire Day Law should have been null and void; he also argued that the law violated the Fourteenth Amendment. Consistent with his earlier rulings on civil rights cases, Harlan admonished the court for its unfairness. He argued that states could, using the same logic in the ruling, make it a crime for blacks and whites to shop at markets and meet together at political rallies.[13]

The legal battle in state and federal courts from 1904 to 1908 also produced parallel campaigns of nonjudicial opposition to the Day Law. In newspapers from Berea to Boston, literate blacks and whites expressed opposition to the Day Law's passage.[14] Even white Berea students who were not always friendly toward black Bereans became opponents of the punitive Day Law that forced the college to expel their peers on racial grounds.[15]

While white Berea students protested the law, black alumni leveled criticism at both the law and President Frost. Blacks criticized Frost for his earlier dismissal of black alumnus James Shelton Hathaway from the college faculty and for the intensified recruitment of whites from Appalachia.[16] Concerned Berea alumni A.W. Titus and Josie Woodford attempted to organize other black alumni against President Frost's exclusion of blacks from the campus. Their anger toward Frost was blunt and direct as they listed the five items to be discussed at a meeting in Lexington on 16 September 1904. Of these, number four was most specific: "4th. Whether or not President Frost is responsible for the present condition of affairs and if responsible shall we publish a letter showing his attitude toward the colored during his entire administration."[17]

Black alumni John T. Robinson, John H. Jackson, Frank L. Williams and J.W. Hughes had all expressed similar misgivings about Frost's leadership, but they failed to speak out against the law and their exclusion. Soon, however, Williams broke the silence by opposing the college trustees' plan to establish a new, all-black version of the college on a separate site.[18]

Black objections to this new, black Berea College received little consideration from the trustees. As early as July 1904, the trustees completed plans to open the school, an act that indicated their acceptance of the permanence of the Day Law. Even before the Supreme Court ruling appeared, the trustees began to select a preliminary site, create a separate endowment to permanently finance it, and develop what they described as a "largely industrial" mission for the new school. The endowment's existence permitted the trustees to create both a fiscal and a physical distance between the two institutions.[19] Moreover, Berea trustees had become convinced that the color line in Kentucky education was an insurmountable reality.

Establishing this separate endowment became a necessity in a state that until the early 1900s had relied largely on privately endowed institutions to provide quality secondary and higher education. Smaller black and white colleges with scant resources struggled while colleges like Berea, the University of Louisville, and Kentucky Wesleyan College persistently attracted larger endowment donations than all other Kentucky schools in the late 1890s and early 1900s.[20] To establish for blacks another school of the quality and stature of Berea required the college trustees to engage in massive fund-raising for this purpose.[21] Ultimately, the trustees set a goal of $400,000 to pay for the construction of an all-black version of Berea College. To raise these funds and legitimize the project, the trustees hired black alumni Kirke Smith and James Bond.

President Frost obtained $350,000 in donations from Andrew Carnegie, Russell Sage, and affluent whites in Boston, Louisville, and New York. According to the stipulation of Andrew Carnegie's $200,000 donation, Kentuckians had to raise $50,000 for the project among themselves. After receiving public support from the Louisville Board of Trade, the state Department of Education, and the *Louisville Courier-Journal,* the Berea fund-raising committee raised $43,000 from local whites and $7,000 from Kentucky blacks.[22]

Throughout this campaign, Kentucky blacks exhibited ambivalent feelings toward the "new Berea." In one incident the Louisville school superintendent, exercising his executive authority, convened a mandatory meeting of Louisville black schoolteachers. Unaware that the meeting was a "new Berea" fund-raising meeting, the teachers gave it their full attention until the white superintendent turned the meeting over to the "Berea [fund-raising] contingent." Black teachers who then recognized the scheme "eased out one by one."[23] Whether they left for financial or political reasons was not clear. It was clear, however, that they left the meeting without making financial contributions to an institution obviously created to sustain racial separation and to enforce the color line.

Black newspaper editor Julia Young supported the teachers' opposition to the "new Berea," arguing that it strengthened the industrial education philosophy.[24] Her editorial opinion was not held by leading white-owned newspapers in the state, nor by all blacks. Her opponents included white publisher "Marse Henry" Watterson of the *Courier-Journal* and black educators at Eckstein Norton Institute of Cane Spring and Chandler Normal School of Lexington, an all-black school affiliated with the American Missionary Association. Each of those schools championed the "new Berea" concept with the presumption that one of them would receive the four-hundred-thousand-dollar endowment. Their endorsements made it appear that the concept had become acceptable to most literate Kentucky blacks.[25]

While Kentucky whites sought a site for the "new Berea," the non-Kentucky white press reported the *Berea* decision as a legal confirmation of racial segregation. Save for editorial condemnations in the *New York Evening Post* and the *Philadelphia Inquirer,* most whites supported the court's protection of racial segregation in education.[26]

In addition to the strengthening of the racial color line in education, the Berea case produced unexpected political turmoil among Kentucky Republicans and their black voters. In 1911 Judge Edward C. O'Rear, who had sided with the Kentucky Court of Appeals majority decision against the college's appeal and indirectly opposed integrated black higher education, decided to run as a Republican candidate for governor. At the beginning of O'Rear's campaign, Democrats, hoping that the state's black voters would vote against O'Rear in the general election, reminded black Republican voters of his role in the Berea case. On the other side, white Republicans provided black Republican campaign workers with enough funds to counteract this effort and encouraged black voters to support O'Rear.[27] Opposed by former governor and populist reformer James

B. McCreary, O'Rear failed to attract enough voters, black or white, and lost by 31,335 votes.[28]

O'Rear's defeat did not, however, reflect well-organized opposition to the philosophy of segregated education. James Bond, a black Berea alumnus and promoter of the "new Berea" idea, claimed that most Kentucky black leaders supported the new school's existence overwhelmingly. On one occasion Bond proclaimed that from Louisville's black leadership alone "Drs. Howser and [J.A.C.] Lattimore, Dr. [L.G.] Jordan, Profs. [Albert Ernest] Meyzeek, McClellan, Lawson, [W.H.] Perry, [J.S.] Cotter, Miss Nannie Burroughs . . . [were] among the largest supporters of the [new Berea] movement."[29] These people represented key religious, fraternal, and cultural elements of Louisville's black community. Bond's announcement of broadly based black leadership support for the "new Berea" school also added credibility to his fund-raising campaign because Burroughs represented a leading black Baptist women's auxiliary organization and Meyzeek, Perry, McClellan, and Lawson held important positions as Louisville public school administrators or teachers. By inference, Bond demonstrated again that key Kentucky black leaders offered qualified but public support for an agency of segregation created by white leaders. This early black support for the "new Berea" allowed whites to conclude that intelligent blacks supported racial segregation as practical public policy. Later, most of the same blacks took a contrary position. Those few Kentucky blacks, such as Julia Young, who had publicly opposed the school from the outset failed to attract widespread black support for a position at odds with the legislative and judicial support for racial segregation.

Significantly, some members of Kentucky's black press, who felt that the approach of white advocates of racial segregated education was moderate and practical, had accepted the wisdom of co-operating with them. Approval from Booker T. Washington and other black leaders on race issues confirmed the wisdom of accepting segregated education. Some blacks, including some in the press, accommodated these opinions by declaring the state "liberal" on race matters. A blatant example occurred in a dispatch from a black

Louisville correspondent to the *Indianapolis Freeman:* "The *Louisville Herald* of August 19 carried on its first page a handsomely ornamented double-column cut showing Governor A.E. Willson and Dr. Booker T. Washington standing together in a characteristic attitude. The publication of such a picture in a leading daily in a city in the border South was the talk of the town. Kentucky holds first place for liberality on the color question [and] recognition of worth, regardless of race."[30]

During the first decade of the century, many of Kentucky's leaders, black and white, accepted racial segregation in education as both practical and necessary for social harmony. At all levels the education color line became a legal mandate and a social policy. With the jewel of formerly integrated education at Berea firmly reserved after 1904 for white mountain youth, white educators and politicians acquiesced to popular racism by hardening the color line in education and made it an integral part of the commonwealth's daily life, following the example of other southern and border states.

2

Acceptance of Civil Racism, 1910-1930

DRAWING THE COLOR LINE in Kentucky higher education appeared simple. But managing industrial education curricula at the various institutions proved far more complex for both white trustees and black administrators. Black educators had to convince their students that industrial education, with its emphasis on vocational education, provided employability but not necessarily equality with whites. Moreover, supporters of black institutions fought white skeptics who distrusted trained black workers. In this setting Kentucky informally supported civil or polite racism that maintained the social order in the finest southern tradition.

This era in Kentucky education followed the incorporation in 1910 of the "new Berea" as Lincoln Institute. Institute administrators and donors promoted the school and its industrial education mission. The campaign to establish the school was both an ideological struggle for the principles of white dominance over black life and an internal battle among black leaders to determine who should lead their race in this nadir period. With conservative, accommodationist blacks already in control, the campaign to expand support for industrial education and Lincoln Institute assumed an important role in Kentucky black life.

Ideological support for Lincoln Institute came from Booker T. Washington, president of Tuskegee Institute in Alabama and the most influential black person of the era. In an effort to maintain his influence in the state, Washington regularly communicated with his Kentucky allies. Among those he wrote expressing support for industrial education at Lincoln Institute were James Shelton Hathaway, president of Kentucky State, L.G. Jordan of the Louisville branch of the National Afro-American Council, publisher William D. Johnson, and influential Lexington minister J.E. Jackson.[1] After Washington's 1906 and 1908 Kentucky speaking engagements, the *Louisville Times* published three "Marse Henry" Watterson editorials promoting Louisville as the school's site. The paper also argued that black industrial education "is of very pertinent interest to the whites of the South and Kentucky."[2]

The juxtaposition of Washington's visits and Watterson's editorials created a positive climate for the philosophical acceptance by leading whites of the new, private all-black industrial school. That acceptance did not guarantee, however, that whites in its vicinity would tolerate such a school. In 1909 whites in the Louisville suburb of Anchorage opposed the proposed placement of Lincoln Institute there. A second site, located twenty-two miles east of Louisville in the town of Simpsonville, generated vigorous opposition from local whites and from nearby Shelbyville. As one measure of their anger, unidentified parties sent two white inspectors of the prospective site "a bundle of switches and hemp rope" and other death threats to persuade Berea agents to stop their inspections. In 1910 John Holland, a state legislator representing Shelbyville and Simpsonville, pushed through the legislature over the governor's veto a law requiring a three-fourths yes vote on the location of industrial schools in a county. The Kentucky Court of Appeals declared the law unconstitutional on the grounds that it violated the state's bill of rights and section 60 of the state constitution, prohibiting a statute that exempted certain classes of cities from its provisions. The court's action permitted the establishment of an industrial school for blacks near Simpsonville.[3]

Although the court abrogated Holland's law, racist interpretations of industrial education in Kentucky black postsecondary education had become entrenched. Many Kentucky blacks saw no hope in opposing this powerful element of segregation.

Not all held such a fatalistic attitude, however; segregated education had its active opponents. The industrial education focus of

Lincoln Institute created an angry reaction from blacks excluded from Berea College by the Day Law.[4] Julia Young, the outspoken editor of the Louisville black weekly, *Kentucky Standard,* argued in January 1909 that the "new Berea" should offer the same curricula provided at Berea College. In a column reporting her perspective in the *Indianapolis Freeman,* Young observed:

> The thing that is puzzling the colored people of this city and state is why is it that the Negro can't have an academic, normal and college training as well as toting the wood and digging the soil. They are asking why is there to be expended $400,000 for a school and the students not given a chance to learn the higher things as well as the industrial pursuits. These things they claim are now taught at the old Berea and why can't they be taught at the new Berea? Such questions are now being asked by the people of city and state and it [is] reported that they must be answered before greater interest will be manifested in the founding of the new institution.[5]

Another less dramatic example of dissatisfaction with using industrial education for segregationist purposes appeared at the 1909 convention of the Kentucky Colored State Teachers Association. The attending principals voted to support the establishment of a college department for Kentucky State, which began as a normal school. Although the proposal went unheeded for thirteen years, their persistent advocacy indicated that some of Kentucky's black educators remained committed to both liberal arts and industrial education for blacks.[6]

In 1915 the liberal arts approach was resurrected by J.W. Bell, an obscure black school teacher from Earlington in western Kentucky, who argued that an important aim of secondary schools should be the preparation of black youth for higher education.[7] Achievement of this goal required a broad liberal arts education rather than a narrowly focused vocational education. Without it, Bell insisted, blacks would be trained only to serve as manual laborers and semiskilled craftsmen.[8]

Other anti-industrial education comments from black Kentucky teachers were rare. Key black educators William J. Simmons and Charles Henry Parrish for example, largely tolerated segregated industrial education. Both men, who received general acclaim for their efforts among black Baptists in Kentucky, were the products of both the slavery and the Reconstruction eras. Simmons, born in slavery in 1849 in Charleston, South Carolina, grew up in Pennsylvania after his mother and two other children escaped. Tutored by his shoemaker uncle in "the common branches," Simmons struggled to find his niche as a dental assistant to white dentist H. De Lange in Bordentown, New Jersey. Denied entry to a dental school, Simmons ran away and joined the Forty-First U.S. Colored Infantry, serving in the Petersburg, Virginia, campaign and in the associated battle of Hatcher's Run. He was present at Lee's surrender at Appomattox Court House.[9]

Following the war, Simmons resumed his dental apprenticeship in New Jersey. He became a member of a white Baptist church there, began to preach, and received support from the congregation to enroll at Madison (Colgate) University, graduating in 1868. He then studied at Rochester University and at Howard University, where he earned his bachelor of arts in 1873.

After teaching in Washington, D.C., and serving as the deputy clerk and county commissioner in Ocala, Florida, he was selected in 1879 to serve as pastor of First Baptist Church, Lexington, Kentucky. In 1882 he was elected editor of a black Baptist church periodical, *The American Baptist*. In 1888 Simmons assumed the presidency of Kentucky Normal and Theological Institute in Louisville, later known as State Colored Baptist University. Simmons, whose national reputation was enhanced by the 1888 biographical anthology *Men of Mark*, used his organizational and fund-raising skills to secure the friendship of Louisville railroad executive Eckstein Norton, whose financial support was later helpful.[10]

While pastor of First Baptist Church, Simmons met Charles Henry Parrish, who emerged as a denominational activist employing the same methods as his own. Born in 1859 and enrolled in local black schools by his parents, Parrish dropped out in 1874 and worked as a porter. He remained interested in education and continued his own after joining the local Baptist church. When Simmons assumed his position at Kentucky Normal and Theological Institute, Parrish followed him there. During his early years at State University, Parrish was an exemplary student, loyal employee, and popular part-time pastor. After earning his bachelor's degree in 1886, Parrish became a delegate to the Republican State Convention, the American National Baptist Convention, and the Committee for the State Normal School, and he assisted Simmons in organizing another school, Eckstein Norton Institute.[11]

Both men had received classical liberal arts collegiate educations, yet both advocated the industrial (vocational) approach as the true path for success for other blacks. Their advocacy of industrial education gave them credibility among powerful white philanthropic agencies and, in turn, respect among fellow blacks for being connected with powerful whites.

Thus, Parrish became an outspoken advocate of industrial education at Eckstein Norton Institute, established in 1890 by Simmons in rural Cane Springs, Kentucky, twenty miles from Louisville. After Simmons's sudden death in late 1890, Parrish assumed the presidency and expanded Eckstein Norton Institute's vocational industrial education curriculum, a step that brought praise from "Marse Henry" Watterson.[12]

Watterson castigated the local elite families of both races, that is, "the smart set of the Colored Four Hundred" and the "Caucasian Four Hundred," for their failure to support efforts by Parrish and Eckstein Norton Institute to educate the presumed intellectually "weaker" black race. Parrish's approach supported the conventional southern wisdom that the institute's graduates would fill jobs subordinate to and unwanted by whites. Although he accommodated segregated education, the state legislature rejected Parrish's appeal for a three-thousand-dollar appropriation for Eckstein Norton.[13]

Unfortunately, Parrish's pleas for support competed with those of James S. Hathaway of Kentucky State, which the legislature had recently renamed the Kentucky Normal and Industrial Institute for Colored Persons. The school, begun in 1886 as a result of lobbying in the state legislature by Parrish, Simmons, and the Kentucky Colored State Teachers Association, promoted itself as the locus of publicly supported industrial education for Kentucky blacks. Its curriculum, composed of programs in teacher training, agriculture, mechanical arts, and business, fit the mold of a Tuskegee Institute–style school.[14]

Ironically, Parrish lobbied for the establishment of the school that later competed with Eckstein Norton Institute for funds and students. He did not anticipate competition from Kentucky State, since Eckstein Norton received the bulk of its funds from private benefactors.[15] Only after William J. Simmons's untimely death in 1890 and a subsequent struggle to enroll students and obtain funds, did Parrish recognize the consequences of his earlier lobbying effort.

James S. Hathaway's aggressive promotion of Kentucky State also undermined Eckstein Norton. Following contact with Booker T. Washington, Hathaway moved away from his liberal arts training at Berea and accepted industrial education as the new pedagogical orthodoxy. This shift may have resulted from his failure to receive a full-time teaching appointment at Berea when blacks were still a part of the campus. Therefore, he competed with Eckstein Norton and Berea by enlarging the industrial element in the Kentucky State curriculum after the school's name change in 1902 to Kentucky Normal and Industrial Institute.[16]

Hathaway's promotion of industrial education at Kentucky State became the central focus of his biennial trustees report. In 1903 he argued that industrial education had become the school's primary instructional mission: "We are pleased with the industrial feature of our school: we wish to extend it as prudence and good judgment may dictate. . . . Students who remain at school here (long enough to catch the inspiration of the place), will not, as a rule, consent to idleness thereafter, but in shop or on farm, will work when and where work can be had. We are especially ambitious to have our own students regarded throughout the state as good and ready workers, just as they are now regarded throughout the state as good and successful teachers."[17] These views confirmed white perceptions that industrial education was the best method to permit blacks to achieve success without stepping beyond their "place" and assured the trustees that Hathaway, as the institute's head, supported an industrial mission.

Hathaway's leadership at Kentucky State temporarily ended in 1907. He resigned the presidency when governor-appointed trustees were going to fire him because of his political affiliation. They then appointed their own man. The departure of Hathaway caused no alteration in the fundamental belief in industrial education for blacks.

His successor, John H. Jackson, had served as president of Kentucky State earlier, from 1886 to 1898. The son of influential black minister Rev. J.E. Jackson of Lexington, he had become convinced of the wisdom of industrial education and the folly for most blacks of obtaining collegiate degrees in classical, liberal arts education. Like Hathaway, Jackson had received his bachelor's degree in liberal arts from Berea College. As a teacher and as the institution's president, he endorsed industrial education, an endorsement that committed the school even more deeply to the industrial education philosophy during his second term (1907-10). Like fellow Berea alumnus Hathaway, Jackson pleaded for more funds to expand facilities and curricula, in order to concentrate on industrial education. He wrote in his 1907 biennial report to the trustees:

> Since the industries have been added and made a part of our regular school work, many students who otherwise, would have had no opportunity to acquire a knowledge of tools, are gradually developing a taste for the same, and are showing a decided tendency towards skilled labor pursuits. . . . But while the outlook for skilled laborers is bright, and while very much of value is being done for those who are doing this character of work, yet I respectfully call your attention to the fact that our mechanical shop is an old frame building, poorly equipped and unsuited for its purpose, if we are to expect better results from such training as is now being given in it. A new shop, built of brick and well equipped for the purpose, would do much to improve the character of the work being done.[18]

Jackson's lamentations about poor manual training facilities under-
stated the limited collegiate and vocational opportunities made available to Kentucky blacks by the state treasury. Those who wanted
more than vocational instruction at Kentucky State had to attend
State University at Louisville or colleges outside the state that allowed black matriculation. By keeping State University nominally
funded via private donations and by providing minimal support for
Kentucky State, white educators upheld Washington's industrial education model as the best way for the black man "to stand
on his feet, to bear his portion of the burdens of the community in
which he lives."[19]

Booker T. Washington's industrial education did not reach all of
the state's major black communities. Frankfort and Louisville blacks
lived closer to the political and economic centers of power and
wealth that supported black industrial education at Lincoln Institute,
Chandler Normal School in Lexington, and Kentucky State.
However, the educational facilities provided to Kentucky blacks in
the western half fell far short of those in the central and eastern sections. Beyond the poorly equipped, all-black, Baptist-operated
Hopkinsville Male and Female College, no significant postsecondary
industrial education institution for western Kentucky blacks operated
until the early 1900s.[20]

In the first decade of the century, blacks received formal education through a polyglot of proprietary and county-supported schools.
Their plight attracted the attention of Dennis Henry Anderson, a
black Tennessean and ordained Colored Methodist Episcopal minister. Following his 1893 graduation from Lane College in Jackson,
Tennessee, Anderson migrated to western Kentucky and established
three independent elementary schools in Fulton and Graves counties.
Seeing the futility of trying to run these poorly equipped schools by
himself, he hoped that the region would support a normal school similar to Kentucky State.

To accomplish this goal, he used his personal funds and a
Paducah lot donated by white businessman Armour Gardner. After
personally digging what he called "a mud hole" for the foundation, in

1909 Anderson opened the West Kentucky Industrial College for Colored Persons (which I will refer to as West Kentucky Industrial) as a proprietary industrial school. Operating from a single wood-frame building, the school initially offered courses in elementary education, agriculture, carpentry, and basic crafts. Revenue came from Anderson's personal finances, tuition payments, and cash contributions from local blacks and whites. When this combination failed to provide sufficient income for Anderson and his wife Artelia Harris Anderson, who served as the school's other teacher, he expanded fund-raising and started a campaign for state support.[21]

In 1912 Anderson lobbied Paducah area state legislators. After he gained their support, they introduced a bill providing the college limited annual funding, but unrelated political disagreements between the governor and west Kentucky politicians interfered, and Governor McCreary vetoed the bill. In the 1914 legislative session, Anderson again lobbied the legislature, urging financial support for West Kentucky Industrial at least equivalent to Kentucky State's support. Despite unanimous support in the Senate, it failed to pass in the House. In 1916 Anderson received strong support from Ernest E. Reed, president of the Kentucky Negro Education Association. By a detailed statistical analysis of black student needs in western Kentucky, Reed tried, unsuccessfully, to convince both houses of the practicality and cost effectiveness of establishing a second black normal school. The Senate again approved the measure but the House voted it down. Finally, in 1918 the legislature passed and the governor signed a law that authorized the Paducah school to operate as "the Booker Washington school of Alabama" did.[22] After six years (1912-18) of struggle with state legislators and governors, West Kentucky Industrial became an integral part of the state's system of segregated institutions of postsecondary education. Anderson's lobbying of the legislature generated an annual state appropriation of three thousand dollars, which provided salaries for himself, his wife, and three other teachers.

In his later biennial pleas for state support, Anderson reiterated his contention that Louisville and Frankfort educators ignored the educational needs of western Kentucky blacks. With western Kentucky legislator backing, he argued successfully for strengthening the school that fulfilled the need for industrial education in that part of the state.

Anderson's accommodation to segregated higher education produced multiple effects. Not only were the annual appropriations of three thousand dollars enlarged, but also Anderson assumed the status of race leader, and with this status dependent on the college presidency, he did not tolerate any black "enemies of the institution."

In one instance Paducah's black Lincoln High School principal suffered Anderson's wrath. The principal, J.H. Alston, had served formerly as an instructor at West Kentucky Industrial. Upon Alston's acceptance of the principalship, Anderson warned him that something serious would happen if Alston did not break away from the local political faction led by Rev. C.C. Carter and F. Harrison Hough, both of whom fell in the "enemies" category.

Shortly thereafter, a black female high school student, Willie Beatty, charged Alston with statutory rape, alleging that he had spent the night with her in a local hotel. In the subsequent trial, a note was produced by the defense in which Beatty demanded five dollars from Alston for her silence. Alston's refusal led to a letter by him to the girl's father, who was a minister in a rival political faction in the town. As the trial progressed, witnesses revealed that Anderson had met with Beatty on several occasions at the school. As the trial ended with acquittal for Alston, it was apparent that Anderson had sought to frame and punish him. Despite descriptions of the incident in the *Pittsburgh Courier,* the entire matter faded from public view shortly thereafter.[23] However, the trial's tawdry revelations tarnished Anderson's image as a statesmanlike leader, clergyman, and educator.

Anderson's reputation also suffered from external evaluations of West Kentucky Industrial management. Reports published in 1921, 1924, and 1932 alleged that the college administration had failed miserably to manage its resources and programs. Moreover, Anderson rejected persistent staff attempts to strengthen the college's weak liberal arts courses and inadequate accounting system.[24]

His adamant support for high school level vocational classes at the college also supported white perceptions that blacks were not ready for true college work. In addition, several incidents of poor fiscal review of college appropriations by its trustees suggested that they cared little about the college's activities as long as the students received training for menial "negro" jobs.[25] Anderson's unvarying co-operation with the trustees allowed him to keep his position despite external dissatisfaction with his job performance and growing internal discomfort with his dictatorial style of management.

Other Kentucky black colleges experienced similar problems of leadership and institutional direction. State University and Kentucky State suffered from persistent financial stringency and from partisan political activities. State University, which absorbed Louisville National Medical College in 1892, Central Law School in 1890, and their collective fiscal problems, began itself to experience financial shortfalls as student needs outstripped campus facilities. Although State University began as a black Baptist-supported normal school, it had evolved by 1918 into a true college with industrial, religious, and liberal arts curricula.

In 1918 Charles Henry Parrish assumed the presidency of State University and persuaded the trustees to change its name to Simmons University (cited hereafter as Simmons) in honor of his mentor and the second university president, William J. Simmons. With this change, Parrish began an aggressive fund-raising campaign among local whites and blacks.

In 1919 a promise by black rest-home operator Dr. James S. Anderson to donate two dollars for every one raised elsewhere encouraged Parrish to begin construction of a new dormitory. But Anderson died suddenly and his estate was declared insolvent, and Simmons did not receive its promised windfall. Meanwhile, the university had overextended itself and had incurred significant long-term debt in order to build dormitories.[26] That debt forced the university to mount a massive fund-raising effort employing a committee of fifty whites from business, government, and churches.[27]

During these fund-raising efforts, a white supporter of Simmons described his view of the university's mission as "service, not race equality."[28] Simmons's course of study produced graduates who would facilitate white control and stereotypes of the "good negro." In accord with such notions, Simmons's choirs performed concerts of "plantation melodies" on the city's first radio station.[29] White supporters of the university had argued earlier that the school helped to uplift blacks but always within the context of careful, white supervision. White campaign manager Rev. R.O. Pirkey wrote in November 1922, "All Southern white people know that the proper training of the Negro, industrially and otherwise, is best handled by their own leaders in the South, assisted and advised from time to time by the Southern white man."[30]

The question of which white men were to provide that advice became important during the first two decades of the twentieth century. Southern whites, including those in Kentucky, struggled to remove corrupt corporate interests from local politics. Large coal companies in eastern Kentucky made the region prosperous but had also become influential in state decision making. Coal companies and railroads were the industrial powers that controlled Kentucky legislators and governors.[31]

After two decades of increasing industrial corporate power in state politics and of the weakening of black voting power by out-migration, black leaders struggled over electoral tactics to achieve maximum effect.[32] Previous Simmons administrators had used secular politics for institutional advancement. In 1883 the General Association of Colored Baptists in Kentucky had sought passage of a special law to establish State Colored Baptist University, Simmons's predecessor. In exchange for the word State in the title, the association had promised each state senator the right to send to the institution, tuition-free, a "properly equipped" student from his district.[33] Simmons used a similar political quid pro quo in its early years.

Consistent with past policy, president Charles Parrish indirectly involved Simmons politically by taking a visible role in Louisville and Kentucky Republican party activities. White Louisville Democrats responded by accusing Simmons students of voting more than once for Republican candidates in each election. Kendrick Lewis, white chairman of the Louisville Democratic Campaign Committee, claimed that forty-four Simmons students cast illegal votes during the 1923 municipal elections.[34] In response, Parrish announced that the university registrar would publish the names of university dormitory residents involved in the controversy.[35] The list revealed that five names cited by Lewis were persons not registered at the school and who had used the school address fraudulently. The other thirty-nine names were not repeat voters. Louisville Democrats complained again in 1926 about this practice.[36] In neither case did the university suffer any immediate repercussions.

It seems likely, however, that Parrish's Republican party participation, among other factors, affected Simmons's long-term fund-raising efforts. Campaigns in 1922 and 1923 failed to produce the expected funds from the mostly white Democrat population of Louisville. The trustees borrowed $60,000 from the Louisville Trust Bank to liquidate lingering debts and underwrite the construction of an $82,760 men's dormitory.[37] But even with the loan, the school remained impoverished. Parrish then reconstituted the bipartisan White Campaign Committee, which included Gov. Edwin P. Morrow, Pres. Frank McVey of the University of Kentucky, Louisville mayor Houston Quin, Democratic politician/businessman Patrick Henry Callahan, and fifty white Louisville businessmen. From 29 May through 19 June 1925, the committee sought $100,000 for Simmons but received only $32,316 from 161 Louisville whites.[38]

When the Simmons University supporters failed to raise sufficient funds and its physical operation appeared threatened, Parrish belatedly asked for support from the Louisville black community. At a 12 July 1925 meeting of two thousand Louisville blacks, he pleaded for, but failed to gain, widespread black financial support.[39]

The failure of Parrish's pleas may have been due to two factors: Simmons had become too closely identified with the Baptist denomination, and he was too intimately connected with a white power structure that championed segregation. For example, Parrish and Louisville Colored Normal School head Albert E. Meyzeek violated a tacit agreement among local black leaders that they would avoid public comment on a proposed city ordinance requiring racial segregation on city streetcars. At a YMCA meeting held at a Baptist church, Parrish and Meyzeek indiscreetly described black behavior on city streetcars as "loud, boisterous and impolite." These comments became additional grist for the mill of prosegregation whites in city government. The next morning, a Louisville white newspaper headline read, "Cause Exists for 'Jim Crow' Law Say Negro Educators."[40]

The Parrish-Meyzeek comments reflected a simmering suspicion by educated blacks that less well-educated blacks were partially responsible for the discriminatory practices imposed on them by whites. Meyzeek and Parrish, as members of the educated elite, experienced racial segregation but by criticizing other blacks escaped some of its debilitating effects. Parrish, for example, was allowed to dine at all-white locations and served as a delegate to the Kentucky Republican Convention and the Republican Committee of Jefferson County. Meyzeek, whose sharp denunciations of racism drew four reprimands from his white supervisors, kept his teaching position when other blacks would have been fired.[41]

Louisville blacks were not the only persons caught up in this web of education, politics, and race. After James S. Hathaway resigned from the Kentucky State presidency in 1907, succeeding president John H. Jackson resigned unexpectedly in 1910. Citing undisclosed "disagreements" with the politically appointed trustees, Jackson's successor, Louisville black educator Meyzeek, also resigned the presidency after only one month in office. According to Meyzeek's biographer, he found "unqualified teachers solidly entrenched through politics" and "filed a frank report of faults and failures with the board of trustees." Louisville blacks and the Louisville school board asked Meyzeek to return as the head of the Louisville Colored Normal School, a makeshift teacher training institution for blacks operated by the Louisville Public Schools.[42]

After Meyzeek's abrupt resignation from Kentucky State, the trustees searched for a less contentious president, one willing to cooperate with them. After appointing Dean Ernest E. Reed interim head, the trustees wrote Booker T. Washington and "other well-known Negro educators of the country, asking them to suggest a Negro for the post of president." The trustees sorted through one hundred nominees and chose former president James Shelton Hathaway, who accepted the position.[43] An advocate of industrial education and Republican orthodoxy, Hathaway avoided confrontations with white trustees and legislators. He failed, however, to avoid problems with the school's black constituents and with the allocation of the meager state appropriations.

The low level of state funding, a subject on which both blacks and whites commented, led to Kentucky State's poor physical condition. Governor McCreary charged in his message to the legislature that the institute suffered from legislator stinginess.[44] Blacks took their concern one step further and began organizing.

In February 1912 a legislative lobbying committee met at the home of Frankfort black attorney L.D. Smith, an intensely partisan black Democrat, who organized a support committee for Kentucky State after revelations of a fiscal crisis at the school.[45] In a later visit to the campus, members of the state legislature "found things in a very bad condition," a direct result of parsimonious funding of the institute. The legislature, however, was little swayed by reports of "things in a . . . bad condition" and voted only $17,500 for Kentucky State, rather than the $50,000 requested in the appropriations bill.[46]

Although the school did make minor improvements with these funds after this crisis, Hathaway's prestige ebbed three months later when newspapers revealed that a prostitution ring operated at the Frankfort black Knights of Pythias hall. Most of the young men patronizing the hall were high school graduates and Kentucky State students. Reports said Hathaway permitted immoral conduct to affect the "better class" of Frankfort's young blacks.[47]

On 6 July 1912 the *Indianapolis Freeman* reported that Hathaway was under public attack for "immorality and incompetence," although, the report continued, the "superintendent [of public instruction] will give him ample time to prove himself innocent."[48] Neither Hathaway nor the superintendent's records revealed the specific nature of these charges. On 17 August 1912 the institute trustees accepted Hathaway's resignation. Hardin Tolbert, publisher of the *Frankfort Tribune* and *Freeman* correspondent, wrote that "the charge against President Hathaway's character was not proven, and it was supposed by many to be the result of politics."[49]

That episode revealed Hathaway's managerial and political weaknesses with regard to the school and black education in general. His perceived failure to exercise complete control over miscreant black students jeopardized his tenure with governor-appointed white trustees. The black citizen–led campaign for increased funding for Kentucky State created an awkward nexus: could legislators increase funding for an already poorly controlled institution? The perceived indiscretions of the students embarrassed other blacks—particularly those in the press—who fought white stereotypes of blacks as lascivious. Ultimately, Hathaway received the brunt of the criticism as the college head. Regardless of culpability, his voluntary departure was welcomed by both blacks and whites.

The controversy surrounding Hathaway's missteps initially made it difficult to hire a replacement. William Buchanon of Alabama Agricultural and Mechanical College and J.H. Garvin of Winchester, Kentucky, both declined the institute presidency.[50] After reviewing nearly two hundred applications for the presidency, including that of past president John H. Jackson, the trustees named black educator and loyal Democrat Green Pinckney Russell of Lexington.[51]

Russell's appointment appeared a logical and politically appropriate choice. A Berea College graduate, he had held the principalship of Lexington's black high school, later named G.P. Russell High School by a school board grateful for his outstanding work and support for the industrial education of blacks.[52] Moreover, recommendations from Democrat state auditor Henry Bosworth and Judge Rodgers Clay gave him an edge over other candidates who were staunch Republicans.

Russell did not fail his white Democrat allies. His willingness to accommodate included tighter control over contentious student behavior. In one nationally publicized incident, several Kentucky State students were reprimanded in 1914 for what the president and trustees labeled "a riot." Some students, including senior James Dean, led students to the campus chapel on 19 October 1914 and condemned Governor McCreary, President Russell, and the trustees for the favoritism shown to the president's nephew, Green P. Russell Jr. Dean, G.P. Russell Jr., and George Parks were accused of smashing the president's automobile. The students involved except Russell's nephew, who allegedly was the chief perpetrator of the mischief, were punished by three weeks of extra manual labor on campus. Dean was expelled for insolent behavior toward a faculty member rather than for this incident.

After convening a meeting of three hundred students in the campus chapel, Dean and his supporters told them that the trustees should remove President Russell because of the board's recent public but minor disagreements with him. Russell responded to the "inflammatory speeches" by inviting local police and the sheriff to the campus to arrest Dean and five other students for disorderly conduct and, in one case, carrying a concealed deadly weapon. A subsequent student boycott also proved unsuccessful; the boycotting students were told to return to classes immediately or be expelled. With no reasonable alternative, the students complied.[53]

Along with his heavy-handed suppression of the October 1914 campus disturbance, Russell displayed a willingness to cooperate with trustees, some of whom wished to become vendors of supplies to the institute. The resulting controversies encouraged Kentucky State alumnus Clarence L. Timberlake to publish a pamphlet implying an improper economic relationship between the trustees and the president.[54] Timberlake argued that the conflict of interest had occurred because Kentucky State confined itself to Franklin County markets and suppliers. The trustees used institute funds to purchase supplies from local vendors regardless of price or quality. As a result the institute served as a vehicle to enrich Franklin county merchants and worked to the detriment of the state's black students, institute staff, and the state treasury.

Timberlake's protests notwithstanding, Russell and the trustees continued to carry out the institute's industrial education mission. But it continued to be hobbled by the legislature's lack of concern for funding even the white schools and colleges. Black education continued to occupy a low rank on the General Assembly's legislative agenda.[55]

As a consequence, Russell's first term at Kentucky State promoted industrial education despite persistent underfunding. During his first term he became more authoritative and his relations with the board of trustees more clouded. In 1921 the state auditor criticized the institute for its mismanagement of state appropriations and federal rehabilitation funds for black war veterans.[56] Russell survived the controversy by winning public support from George Colvin, chairman of the Kentucky State trustees and superintendent of public instruction.[57]

Two years later Colvin sought the governorship. Because he needed the help of the black Republican leadership, he agreed that a black Republican should again become president of Kentucky State. Colvin therefore had to remove Russell without seeming to compromise his 1921 endorsement. When outgoing governor Edwin P. Morrow did not appoint another Democrat to fill a vacancy on the Kentucky State board of trustees, Colvin and two Republican trustees maneuvered to remove Russell from his position as president.[58]

In closed sessions, the trustees created a rationale for Russell's ouster. Colvin and the trustees alluded to low student morale and a weakening of the institute's management. Blaming Russell for these conditions, the board voted not to rehire him for the 1923-24 academic year. Immediately, the trustees selected an institute staff member, Francis Marion Wood, to serve as president.[59]

The selection of Wood was based on political considerations rather than academic criteria. Wood was the brother of John E. Wood, publisher of the black weekly *Danville Torchlight* and member of the Kentucky state Republican committee. John Wood also exercised indirect political influence by serving as the moderator (president) of the General Association of Colored Baptists in Kentucky, the largest black Baptist organization in a state where the Baptist denomination was paramount among black worshipers and voters. After F.M. Wood's presidential appointment, Colvin assumed that John Wood would provide an endorsement to his readers and to General Association congregations.[60]

Russell publicly objected to his dismissal and Wood's appointment by exposing Colvin's scheme and by arguing that Colvin should have fired him "if I was incompetent as he says I was." Russell also argued that Colvin waited to act until "negro politicians" had told him that Russell's removal had become the price for their support.[61] Russell then received letters suggesting that however much black Republicans liked Colvin, black voters wanted better education than the institute's Republican president could provide. Russell's perceptions of black voter preferences proved correct: Colvin's bid for the governorship failed.[62]

As for Russell, he waited for the political winds to change with the arrival of new Kentucky State trustee appointments. Incoming Democratic governor William Jason Fields named new Democratic trustees to the college's board. Pres. F.M. Wood, following Colvin's suggestion, introduced a junior college program and continued the existing industrial education courses. Beyond this improvement, Wood, an institute staff member and 1904 alumnus, made few changes in Kentucky State. For the remainder of the 1923-24 academic year, Wood served as a lame-duck administrator because the new board had decided to restore Russell to the presidency on 1 July 1924. Wood later moved to Baltimore, Maryland, where he obtained a fellowship to study at Morgan State College. After appointment as supervisor of the city's fifteen black public schools, he remained active in that position until his death on 8 May 1943.[63]

The Wood-Russell era at Kentucky State had amply shown that public black institutions of higher education too often served as platforms for white political advancement and agencies for black voter manipulation.

Russell's controversial presidential terms occurred during a period of heightened expectations for improvement in all of Kentucky black higher education, especially in Louisville. In 1920 white educators asked a committee of black educators and citizens to promote a bond issue for the improvement of the all-white University of Louisville and the city public schools. Following an unsatisfactorily vague remark by the white bond issue committee that local black education needs would be "taken care of," the black committee refused to support the bond issue's passage.[64] Louisville blacks recognized the need to exert themselves to extract concessions from indifferent whites. Irritated by their curt treatment, the ad hoc committee of Louisville blacks (excluding Pres. Charles H. Parrish and William Steward of Simmons University, who supported the bond issue) acquired the support of an influential, wealthy white Democrat and social activist. Patrick Henry Callahan, who had earlier opposed anti-Catholic and anti-immigrant activities in Kentucky, now took on the struggle because he recognized that strong Republican support for it and the bond issue's benefits excluded blacks. The committee publicized its opposition and developed a coalition of black and white voters that produced a four-thousand-vote margin to defeat the bond issue in the November 1920 general election.[65]

This moment of biracial electoral cooperation over the bond issue provided younger black leaders I. Willis Cole, William Warley, and Wilson Lovett an opportunity to develop their political skills. A rump group of these black Republicans decided to field a slate of fifteen opposition candidates for citywide offices. Opposed by Charles Parrish, Albert E. Meyzeek, and other conservative black Republicans, the 1921 Lincoln Independent Party (LIP) slate indicated that some Louisville blacks continued the activism begun in the 1920 bond issue campaign. As the campaign evolved, it took on an ominous tone when the businesses of LIP candidates suffered vandalism and the candidates themselves were harassed by black underworld figures allegedly hired by political opponents.[66]

Although the LIP failed to elect a single candidate, it forced the older, educated black leaders to relinquish control to the younger ones. Conservative leaders Parrish and Meyzeek could no longer claim to speak for their community. Parrish, whose fiscal woes at Simmons would soon begin to overwhelm him, had to share his race leadership with Cole, Warley, and others. That gradual redistribution of race leadership coincided with the 1925 resurrection of the University of Louisville bond issue. The university recognized that black voter support was essential for passage. In a concession to the black ad hoc committee, the university agreed to reserve one-sixth of the $1 million proceeds ($166,000) for the improvement of Louisville black education.[67]

With black support assured, the bond issue received approval in the November 1925 general election. After the election, however, the university virtually ignored its oral commitment to the black education project. University of Louisville presidents George Colvin and John Patterson concentrated instead on refurbishing campus buildings, restructuring the administration, and reorganizing curricula. This situation continued for four years while the black leadership grew more and more impatient with their dilatory treatment by the white leadership. In late 1929 the university proposed the organization of a black junior college. Of the one hundred thousand dollars set aside for this purpose, thirty-five thousand to forty thousand dollars would be used to purchase the building, and the remainder would go for equipment. The other sixty-six thousand dollars promised in 1925 had been deleted by the university. The ad hoc black leadership committee rejected this proposal.[68] As a stopgap the university granted two thousand dollars to Simmons for "extension courses" for blacks. Given the unfulfilled political and fiscal assurances made in 1925, this temporary measure did little to satisfy Louisville's black leaders.

Louisville blacks were not the only ones who felt the continuing effects of politics on the fortunes of education. The most glaring example occurred at Kentucky State after the 1924 reappointment of Green P. Russell. Russell's resumption of power meant a continuation of the industrial education tradition, limited state appropriations, and close cooperation with white Democrat trustees and their political cronies.

His administration remained uneventful until 1926, when several significant episodes occurred. A disastrous dormitory fire in which three students died forced the institute trustees to request $184,000 from the legislature in order to rebuild; the state legislature approved a special appropriation to cover the cost. Subsequently, at the trustees' request, the legislature changed the legal name of Kentucky State to Kentucky State Industrial College for Colored Persons to reflect the introduction of a new, four-year liberal arts college program. Such a move followed the national and regional trend to create liberal arts colleges for blacks, since industrial jobs once held by blacks were becoming more acceptable to unemployed whites. Moreover, public schools were requiring their teachers to have collegiate rather than normal school preparation. Also, in a move sparked by electoral promises of the reform of state government, the legislature limited the Kentucky State president's term of office to four years. An earlier statute had permitted it to be indefinite.[69]

Shortly after passage of this law, Gov. Flem Sampson appointed H.D. Martin and J.M. Perkins to replace members of the board of trustees whose terms had expired. Both men expressed suspicions about Russell's management of the college accounts. As a result the board hired its own accountant, E.R. Burch, to audit the college's fiscal condition. His investigation revealed, among other problems, that Russell had conspired with previous white Democratic trustees to misuse the college's state appropriations. As an example of this collusion, Burch cited Russell's hiring of his wife and his daughter as librarians for the college library of two hundred books. In response Russell argued that hiring his wife and his daughter had saved the college money. The trustees remained skeptical.[70]

The trustees' distrust encompassed nearly the entire college staff and institutional operations. They questioned Russell's hiring of senior college students as faculty and, shortly thereafter, asked for the students' resignations. At the end of lengthy and intense questioning, the trustees finally asked for Russell's resignation on 20 February 1929. After some hesitation, he resigned effective 1 March 1929, and Dean James A. Bond was appointed as interim college head.[71]

Russell was indicted on three counts of defrauding the state by paying his wife and his daughter for their campus duties.[72] In his legal defense Russell received support from former trustees, and the prosecutor failed to persuade Burch to come from New Orleans to testify and thus strengthen the prosecution's case. Given Russell's strong character references, the absence of a witness to provide evidence against him, and a second continuance of the trial, the judge dismissed the case.[73] Again, Russell had survived. He moved to Waukegon, Illinois, to join his married daughter and dentist son-in-law. There he worked in the public schools, became a respected citizen, and remained active in local Democratic politics until his death in 1936.[74]

Russell's resignation at Kentucky State, the fiscal and political troubles of Charles H. Parrish at Simmons, and the growing disillusionment of some whites with Dennis H. Anderson at West Kentucky Industrial were similar in several dimensions. All three college presidents exercised political clout not directly related to education. As a result each president had to contend with two institutional constituencies: an internal one comprised of faculty, staff, and alumni and an external group made up of the governing boards and the state legislature. The latter group, composed of whites, remained generally unconcerned about day-to-day operations unless malfeasance or nonfeasance appeared. The students became dependent on the president's recommendations in order to obtain their degrees and to find employment thereafter.

This saga again denies any student or community roles in the process. After the 1914 incident in which several student protestors were arrested by local police on the order of President Russell and later expelled, Kentucky State students remained suspicious of its administrative leadership. The president and his family lived in a brick home and received abundant food from the school farm, while students were constrained to live in poorly insulated, wood frame buildings and were fed inadequate meals. Under each administration before 1929, the presidents implored the trustees to improve campus facilities and also to raise the meager staff salaries. Student concerns about campus conditions were addressed only infrequently by the administrators.

Meanwhile, white educators continued to advocate the classical, liberal arts curricula for white collegians, and black educators grew increasingly distrustful of the industrial education curricula. Attempting to resist these changes, industrial education advocates argued unsuccessfully that black industrial education schools better served the needs of most blacks. Because black higher education had become more acceptable to whites as part of the public education mission, the creation in the 1920s of local college programs for blacks had indirectly confirmed the inadequacy of industrial education as the primary direction for black postsecondary education. Many black secondary schools, however, continued to be dominated by vocational education curricula.

This change in educational philosophy for black colleges coincided with the expansion of black postsecondary education in the South. In the Reconstruction era, blacks could choose from a handful of southern institutions that offered them college level work. In 1927 the number had increased to eighty-two. Although most were poorly equipped in comparison with southern white colleges, southern white acceptance of black colleges demonstrated that the educated black elite fulfilled leadership roles within segregated southern society.[75]

Southern whites, however, kept those schools inferior in scope and thus circumscribed black participation in the institutional and intellectual growth of the region. Southern black higher education sustained only two viable medical schools—Meharry Medical College and Howard University School of Medicine. Howard University had the only law school. State University's law and medical programs had disappeared by 1920. Engineering and business programs were limited to courses in drafting and bookkeeping. At the end of the first two decades of this century, only a dozen southern black colleges offered programs in these professional areas that were comparable to those at small, southern white colleges.[76]

Such conditions resulted from Kentucky whites' efforts to operate higher education for blacks as no more than an afterthought. Chronic pleas for funds for black public and private institutions were given minimal attention until crises forced state legislators or private donors to provide nominal funds.

In this context the formative period of black higher education in Kentucky from 1910 to 1930 prepared blacks for specific racial roles and ignored black intellectual and professional growth. What little black higher education existed in these decades confirmed the Day Law's requirement for separate black education and the assignment of blacks to a subordinate status. Whites expected postsecondary industrial education to emphasize vocational/industrial education that limited blacks to low-paying, semiskilled jobs in agriculture, domestic service, and crafts. Other types of jobs were rare or unlikely for most blacks. Given these assumptions, white politicians and philanthropists, eager not to disrupt the racial status quo, justified both the philosophy and the funding of industrial education through 1930. With few exceptions, black educators in Kentucky accepted this state of affairs as a fait accompli.

Clearly, institutions of black higher education from 1910 to 1930 had become systemic agents for the maintenance of racial segregation. What reforms Kentucky's black educators expected to make as the system shifted from an industrial education to a liberal arts focus became more problematic after 1930. That year marked the strengthening of Kentucky State, the continuing deterioration of West Kentucky Industrial, and the opening of a new black college in Louisville. As usual, Kentucky's black educators adjusted to these changes. But the deepening national depression that began in 1929 further complicated educational reform, as leaders in Kentucky and in the nation concentrated on ending the "hard times" rather than on improving schools and colleges.

3

Hopes, Reforms, and Resistance, 1930-1939

As the nation reacted to the financial turmoil following the stock market collapse of October 1929, black educators and race leaders sorted out their cautious responses to white demands for efficiency and quality in the operation of black educational institutions. Since 1921 black educators in the state colleges had been attacked for inefficient management and poor quality of instruction under their separate but unequal status.

Changing this arrangement took on quixotic dimensions. If black educators persuaded their governing boards to make reforms in curricula and management, any adjustments had to conform to educational theories acceptable to white educators usually unfamiliar with life on black college campuses. If black Kentucky students declined to participate in this segregated system, then they had to go elsewhere—presumably out of the state—for desegregated and presumably better higher education.

Complicating these conditions, Kentucky's black institutions of higher education were compelled to adapt to shifting national educational trends. In 1928 and 1930 the U.S. Office of Education published studies that described (and indirectly supported) contemporary approaches to black higher education. In place of the industrial education promoted in earlier decades by Booker T. Washington and others, liberal arts curricula that emphasized the fine arts and sciences had appeared in many black normal and even industrial schools. As a result some of these schools became "colleges for Negroes" that offered blacks both vocational skills and liberal arts programs leading to teaching certificates. Legitimating these institutions among blacks and suspicious whites often became problematic in southern states. The unsuccessful struggle to convince Kentucky blacks that Lincoln Institute ought to be like Berea rather than an outright industrial school exemplified this problem.

The difficulty of making these institutions academically credible was also compounded by personnel and institutional upheavals. For example, after the forced ouster of Pres. Green P. Russell, Kentucky State trustees elected a new president who was mandated to develop a fiscally efficient and academically sound institution. Louisville black educators and community leaders witnessed the swift deconstruction of Simmons University from a comprehensive private liberal arts college for Kentucky blacks to a denominational Bible college. Following a painful campaign to gain state support, West Kentucky Industrial's administrators fostered a nagging public perception of corruption and chronic ineptitude at the helm.

Yet, these higher education institutions, while functioning as institutional agents for a racially segregated society, produced positive economic and political changes—however subtle—within that structure. The best example of that process occurred in Louisville in 1930. The ad hoc committee for Louisville black education visited new University of Louisville president Raymond Kent in July 1929, wanting to know how the university intended to provide promised opportunities in higher education.[1] Declining to answer their demands immediately, President Kent brought their concerns before the trustees. To resolve this problem, the University of Louisville and Simmons University trustees negotiated the sale of the existing Simmons campus to the University of Louisville. Simmons paid off its outstanding long-term debts with the proceeds. As a part of the agreement, Simmons's trustees halted its collegiate level programs. Students who would have enrolled in Simmons's collegiate curricula could enroll at the proposed Louisville Municipal College for Negroes, an all-black, physically separate liberal arts unit of the University of Louisville. As for Simmons, the agreement permitted it to function as a Baptist Bible college using one of the old Simmons University buildings until Louisville Municipal needed it. In the interim, Simmons trustees worked to relocate to a new campus site in west Louisville.[2]

These events were the culmination of black political pressure that began in 1920, directed toward the foundation of a nondenominational public college for Louisville blacks. In 1931 Louisville Municipal opened with fifty students and seven faculty members. All of the faculty had graduate training from non-Kentucky universities—a first among Kentucky black colleges.[3] Although Louisville Municipal also began as a two-year college with a liberal arts orientation, within four years the University of Kentucky placed Louisville Municipal on its list of approved state institutions. Blacks could not enroll at the University of Kentucky, but it would have accepted academic credits from Louisville Municipal if blacks had been able to enroll. With this recognition from the University of Kentucky and with the University of Louisville president Kent's claim that the school was the only liberal arts municipal college for blacks in the country, Louisville Municipal quickly attracted additional students from the local black community.

While Louisville blacks welcomed their inclusion—albeit segregated—within the University of Louisville, other Kentucky black colleges struggled continuously for improved facilities and for equity in the funds allocated to them. These problems intensified as Kentucky State's new president, Rufus Ballard Atwood, worked to end the school's traditional entanglement with Kentucky partisan politics and to fulfill the trustees' mandate for institutional efficiency.[4]

Atwood, a native of tiny Hickman, Kentucky, and a black war hero, was no stranger to difficult situations. During World War One he received several battlefield commendations for bravery, including the Bronze Star. Upon his return from overseas duty, he earned bachelor's degrees from Fisk University (1920) and Iowa State College (1923) and served briefly as professor of agriculture at Kansas Vocational College and then as professor and dean of the Prairie View Agricultural and Mechanical College in Texas from 1923 until his selection for the Kentucky State presidency in 1929. In his first months in office, he fired faculty and staff who had been hired on the basis of political connections.[5]

Atwood established for the college an academic mission that placed greater emphasis on the liberal arts and teacher preparation than on industrial education. Because this mission required competent faculty, one of Atwood's first actions as president was to not renew the teaching contracts of fourth-year college students who served as part-time instructors. Instead, he sought out and hired instructors with master's and doctor's degrees from integrated universities outside the South. Atwood's forceful actions revived a moribund campus wracked by cronyism, overt intrusion by white politicians, and student suspicion of the administration. His nonpartisan approach to education strengthened his presidency and the college's integrity and academic credibility.

Unlike his predecessor, Green P. Russell, Atwood had prepared himself by eschewing any overt Kentucky political connections. The trustees who fired Russell wanted a replacement who had no connections with the state's Republican or Democratic parties. Although his father, Pomp Atwood, served on the city of Mayfield's black school board, Rufus Atwood avoided any overt local or regional partisan political activity. Moreover, he registered later as an independent, which excused him from participating in the hotly contested Republican and Democratic primary elections.[6] To circumvent partisanship in staff appointments, he relied on contacts made when he was appointed in 1931 as the secretary of the Association of the Negro Land Grant Colleges. His experiences enabled him to resolve the multiple problems faced by a southern black college, including that of academic integrity.[7]

Atwood's endeavor to remove Kentucky State from Kentucky politics coincided with efforts in Kentucky higher education to overcome general fiscal deprivation. In the depression era of the 1930s, the state's public higher education institutions struggled to operate with fewer dollars. To reduce waste in education, the state wanted to tighten its control over the semiautonomous white teachers colleges and the state university.

In the 1930-39 decade Kentucky, Indiana, and Rhode Island adopted reorganization plans according to which the governing boards of white state-supported colleges were nominally attached to a state administrative department.[8] This change affected white institutions at a time when total enrollments were dropping. For example, Western Kentucky State Teachers College lost 22.3 percent of its students between 1931-32 and 1933-34. Faculty members at other white state-supported colleges were also affected. At Murray State Teachers College the total number of faculty declined by 22 percent between 1931-32 and 1933-34.[9] Such losses in students and faculty undermined the operations of these institutions during the depression years.

Black higher education, too, fell victim to the depression. The Kentucky State faculty suffered during the early depression years as state funding became scarce. In the 1931-32 academic year Kentucky State had thirty-four full-time faculty. By 1933-34 the number had dropped to twenty-six, and although there were fewer Kentucky State teachers, student enrollment at the college increased by 56 percent from 1931-32 to 1933-34.[10] Kentucky blacks, including those in Louisville, continued to enroll at the older Kentucky State rather than Louisville Municipal.[11] With a new institution and an increased national emphasis on liberal arts education, more blacks sought out advanced education. However, white student enrollments declined, aggravated by the fiscal and faculty reductions at the teachers college and the state university. Although all Kentucky campuses were faced with serious challenges, black students responded to their campus conditions more positively. Unlike President Russell, Atwood defused student opposition and established in 1929, with the students, a pattern of campus reform and administrative cooperation.[12] In 1932 the college administration permitted the students to edit (with an advisor's oversight), publish, and finance the *Thorobred*, a campus newspaper started in 1929.[13] Previously, the college had exercised complete control of student expression. For the next three decades this newspaper reflected the opinions of literate students who fiercely defended the college family, including faculty and staff.[14]

The close-knit character of the college originated only in part from Atwood's leadership, for Kentucky State also developed a strong intercollegiate athletics program under Henry Arthur Kean, a student of Notre Dame's outstanding coach Knute Rockne. In 1934 and 1937, the Frankfort college was recognized as the unofficial national football champion among black colleges.

Under Atwood's leadership the campus became an intellectual oasis as outstanding black thinkers visited it. Among them were W.E.B. Du Bois (in 1940), Mary McCleod Bethune (1941), Zora Neal Hurston (1942), Langston Hughes (1943, 1951, and 1960), and Walter White (1946).[15]

The college had also made important qualitative changes in curricula. The central focus remained on teacher education, but Atwood introduced distinct departments for the three areas: natural science and mathematics (in 1929); agriculture, sociology, and economics (in 1931); and health and physical education (in 1931). The remaining departments—music, education, home economics, English, and foreign languages—offered bachelor's degree programs that had been unavailable prior to 1929.[16] Within the restrictions of Kentucky's segregated education law, the college also attracted academically accomplished black men and women who came to the campus as junior faculty with earned bachelor's degrees and subsequently earned master's and doctoral degrees from out-of-state universities. In the 1929-39 decade, 50 percent of the Kentucky State faculty pursued further graduate training.[17] Setting the example was President Atwood, who used summer leaves of absence to earn a master's degree in education administration in 1939 from the University of Chicago. By 1939 46 percent of the faculty had earned at least master's degrees, and 16 percent had earned doctorates.[18]

The academic advances made at Kentucky State and Louisville Municipal had profound effects on both schools. The Southern Association of Colleges and Secondary Schools assigned a B rating to Kentucky State in 1931 and Louisville Municipal in December 1935. That meant that graduates of the two schools had received approved bachelor's degrees, but the degrees were not equal to those received at white colleges. In 1937 the association ranked Louisville Municipal A, indicating that the college was meeting the standards of white colleges. In 1939 the association changed Kentucky State's 1931 rank of B to A as well.[19]

While Louisville Municipal was developing into a strong liberal arts college, the college's dean, Dr. Rufus Clement, resigned in 1936 to become the president of the private, black research-oriented Atlanta University.[20] The former dean of West Virginia State College for Negroes, David A. Lane, assumed the Louisville Municipal deanship and continued to pursue the college's liberal arts mission.[21]

The decade-long evolution of Kentucky State and Louisville Municipal into effective institutions overshadowed the decline of Kentucky's smallest state supported college for blacks, West Kentucky Industrial College. Revelations about its poor financial condition and inadequate campus facilities continued to make it less attractive to west Kentucky blacks. In 1931 and 1932 West Kentucky Industrial came under fire from the state auditor and the University of Kentucky School Service Bureau for poor fiscal management. The college also received criticism in a legislature-commissioned efficiency study of Kentucky state government.[22] The all-white study team, after evaluating all agencies of state government, criticized West Kentucky Industrial heavily for its inadequate bookkeeping system and its poorly trained faculty and staff.[23]

Despite that criticism, Dennis H. Anderson remained as president. He held on because he accommodated the needs of Paducah's white elite. In 1936, for example, he supported a bond issue for Paducah Junior College, which blacks could not attend; his willingness to promote the bond issue among Paducah's black voters endeared him to white politicians and educators.[24]

Although grateful, Paducah's white leaders were only at first willing to renew their support for Anderson. Other actions during the decade from 1926 to 1936 began to undermine support for West Kentucky Industrial from both blacks and whites. Poorly prepared faculty, insufficient income from the college farm, and low student morale created serious new doubts. Western Kentucky blacks observed these problems and chose to attend Kentucky State instead.[25]

Anderson's resistance to change also discouraged some staff members who sought improvements. In one case, Dean George D. Wilson left West Kentucky Industrial, citing Anderson's intransigence as the reason. Later, he became a faculty member at Louisville Municipal.[26]

With conditions deteriorating, the trustees decided in 1935 to assume for themselves most of Anderson's duties and responsibilities, leaving him only his title as president.[27] But their management of campus life was not much better. Students resorted to desperate means to resolve a dispute over student life policies. In December 1936 the student body refused to attend classes, citing college prohibitions against males walking with females from classrooms to the dining hall, visitation privileges, and Sunday church escorts. The faculty yielded to the demands for change and the strike ended.[28]

In 1937 Anderson was removed as titular president. To replace him, the trustees selected Harvey Clarence Russell, a Simmons University and University of Cincinnati graduate who had been the dean at Kentucky State. Russell immediately began to introduce curricular and administrative reforms similar to those enforced at Kentucky State by Atwood.[29]

As the trustees of West Kentucky Industrial implemented Russell's reforms, prominent Kentucky blacks became concerned about the declining quality of all higher education. One of these persons, Charles W. Anderson Jr. of Louisville, became a central figure in Kentucky black politics from 1935 to his untimely death in 1960. In 1935 Louisville and Jefferson County Republicans nominated Anderson to represent the predominantly black Forty-Second State Legislative District. Local Democrats supported black attorney C. Eubank Tucker, but Anderson, a young lawyer in his first political campaign, easily defeated him, assisted by Tucker's opposition to the Louisville Urban League's civil rights campaigns.[30]

Anderson's election to a state legislature was the first of a southern black since Reconstruction. As the state's only black legislator, he won approval in the 1936 legislative session for a law that provided Kentucky black college graduates with tuition grants for out-of-state graduate and professional education. This action was remarkable because the Supreme Court in *Murray v. University of Maryland* had voided Maryland's use of such grants to escape creating separate graduate and professional schools. Just as surprising, the national NAACP legal advisory committee, of which Anderson was a member, withheld criticism of the Kentucky legislator's action.[31]

The Anderson-Mayer Student Aid Law had forced white Kentucky legislators to contend with the absence of graduate and professional training for blacks in its segregated educational structure.[32] The law's passage also exposed the failure of the governance board of Kentucky's black colleges to create comprehensive college-level institutions while sustaining the requirements of the Day Law. Awarding out-of-state tuition grants did, however, temporarily thwart lawsuits by blacks ready to argue that the state provided them unequal higher education.

Anderson's legislation allowed Kentucky white educators to continue their neglect of black higher education. At the same time, criticism of West Kentucky Industrial and Kentucky State revealed doubts by white educators and politicians in state government about the viability of these schools as distinct institutions. Such questions melded with a gradual, national philosophical shift from industrial education to liberal arts as the key instructional approach for black colleges. Editorials in the *Chicago Defender* and the *Pittsburgh Courier* questioned the competence of black colleges to "adjust curricula to adequately prepare graduates to properly find their place in life."[33] Hence, even black critics appeared to corroborate Kentucky whites' criticism that black colleges were often weak and industrially oriented. By inference, black colleges created to support industrial education had become anachronisms in need of reinvention.

Such revelations in the midst of a national economic depression and a shift of black voter allegiance from the Republican to the Democratic Party prompted white politicians to press for subtle changes in Kentucky black higher education. The chief white proponent of these changes was the controversial populist governor, Albert Benjamin Chandler.

Elected in 1935 with a mandate to reform Kentucky's corrupt political system, Chandler completed the reorganization of state government as directed by the 1934 session of the legislature.[34] The control of Kentucky State and West Kentucky Industrial was shifted to the State Board of Education, thereby centralizing the oversight of two institutions with a recent history of poor fiscal management. Intended as a reform measure, this section of the reorganization law had important implications for black higher education. President Atwood believed that the change removed Kentucky black colleges from politics by placing them under the control of the less partisan state board. It had the effect, however, of associating black higher education with elementary and secondary education.

In 1935 public criticism of Kentucky's black colleges had begun to resurface, particularly after continuing difficulties at the Paducah college. Governor Chandler's concern focused primarily on the positive developments at Kentucky State. Both Chandler and Kentucky State president Atwood were born and raised in small western Kentucky towns; their wives both had Virginia backgrounds. Recognizing their similarities, including the reformist philosophies that they held in common, Atwood established a cordial but discreet friendship with Chandler. That relationship manifested itself in the 1937-38 dispute over the closure of West Kentucky Industrial.

The controversy began when Dennis H. Anderson's successor, Harvey Clarence Russell, made substantial progress in correcting deficiencies at West Kentucky Industrial. Despite Russell's efforts, Governor Chandler announced in a December 1937 meeting with Louisville black leaders that he wanted to close the Paducah school and assign the property to other state agencies. He proposed that Kentucky State become a "high-type institution in Frankfort."[35] This proposal met with stiff opposition from black educators, race leaders, and white western Kentucky politicians, including Paducah state representative Henry Ward and the Paducah board of trade.[36]

Some members of the Kentucky Negro Education Association (KNEA) argued that black students needed more, not fewer, higher education institutions if Kentucky's segregated system was to offer blacks truly equal education. Other KNEA members, including Atwood, supported Chandler's view and cited data showing that western Kentucky black students preferred to attend the stronger and better organized Kentucky State.[37]

On top of black educator disarray, Charles Anderson refused Chandler's request to introduce the merger bill.[38] After extended discussion and lobbying by West Kentucky Industrial backers and promerger advocates Chandler and Atwood, western Kentucky legislators Henry Ward and Clyde Lester joined Charles Anderson to introduce a compromise bill that, upon subsequent passage, gave both sides something. As originally proposed by Chandler, West Kentucky Industrial closed on 30 June 1938. But as a concession to western Kentucky blacks and their white allies, it reopened on 1 July 1938 as West Kentucky Vocational School for Negroes (WKVSN) with a clearly defined vocational mission.

The law also shifted all liberal arts courses to the Frankfort college. Since Kentucky State no longer focused primarily on industrial education, domestic science, agriculture, or mechanics, it became, on 1 July 1938, the Kentucky State College for Negroes, the sole provider of state-supported higher education for blacks in Kentucky.[39] This law did not affect Louisville Municipal, which continued to function as a segregated unit of the private but municipally supported University of Louisville.

The process of transforming the Frankfort and Paducah institutions tarnished Chandler's reputation among blacks. Chandler argued that he had improved black educational opportunities by creating a "new" black vocational school. He also contended that higher education evaluators had, since 1923, cited the absence of this type of school as a deficiency in the state system.[40]

The effects of these changes were not immediately noticeable in Kentucky black higher education. Atwood felt, however, that the controversy strengthened the personal friendship between himself and Chandler. He remained a covert ally of Chandler and of others in the Chandler faction of the Kentucky Democratic party. Using political aplomb, Atwood made it appear that Kentucky State received no tangible, direct benefits from the relationship.[41]

The merger controversy erupted in a period when southern higher education as a whole lagged far behind higher education in the rest of the nation. Southern white colleges did not rank with the leading institutions of higher education. To remedy this, national studies of higher education encouraged southern colleges to introduce stronger liberal arts and science curricula and to move away from normal schools to four-year teachers colleges and comprehensive colleges, universities, and professional schools.[42]

The scarcity of education dollars from private donors and state legislatures postponed the immediate introduction of those changes. Kentucky, which had benefited from the 1920s prosperity of "King Coal" in eastern Kentucky, struggled to maintain public services with slim depression-era tax revenues. Unsuccessful efforts to introduce a sales tax and a $75 million revenue bond issue delayed needed improvements in Kentucky education and other social services. White colleges and the state university at Lexington, moreover, had become the first priority for improvement; black higher education again received far less attention.[43]

Faced with meager public support from whites, Kentucky's black colleges also had to contend with a growing national criticism of black higher education.[44] Such black critics as James Weldon Johnson, Charles H. Thompson, and W.E.B. Du Bois wanted black colleges to redefine their missions and specify what kind of institutions black students needed to survive in a racially hostile society.[45] At one point those critics proposed consolidation or closure of the smaller, weaker black colleges.[46] That position seemed to strengthen President Atwood's support for the transformation of West Kentucky Industrial into a vocational school and to undermine anti-merger opponents. Atwood also supported the replacement of Kentucky State's industrial education courses with liberal arts curricula. Louisville Municipal, under Dean Rufus Clement until 1936, had included few industrial education courses. A commuter student institution, Louisville Municipal emphasized humanities and science degree programs in its curricula, with one- and two-year programs in limited vocational areas. Even in those programs, the black instructors had earned master's degrees and doctorates.[47]

The hiring of credentialed faculty at Louisville Municipal prompted Kentucky State to follow suit. In 1929 six (28.5 percent) of the Kentucky State faculty had no degrees, fourteen (66.66 percent) had bachelor's degrees, and only one person (4.76 percent) had a master's degree. No faculty members had yet earned a doctorate.[48] By the 1938-39 academic year, ten (38.47 percent) of the Kentucky State faculty had bachelor's degrees, twelve (46.15 percent) had master's degrees, and four (15.38 percent) had earned doctorates. Of the latter four, one degree was in the natural sciences, one in mathematics, one in agriculture, and one in education. The college put pressure on faculty without master's degrees to earn them during the summer breaks.[49]

By 1938 all Kentucky black higher education emphasized liberal arts curricula that led to teacher certification. At the same time, its institutions gradually improved their academic integrity and instructional quality. These improvements at Kentucky State and similar programs at Louisville Municipal enlarged the in-state college offerings. Also, under the governance of the nonpartisan State Board of Education, black higher education offered truly collegiate-level curricula and without the scandals of previous decades. Such a governance system was not intended for white colleges since black ones were never presumed to be their equal.

Based on the changes since 1929, black higher education had made perceptible improvements, but a few black educators and race activists remained unconvinced that the system had become philosophically or financially equal to that provided whites. Led by Louisville school teacher Lyman T. Johnson and by publisher I. Willis Cole of the *Louisville Leader* newspaper, an informal group of fifteen Louisville blacks met regularly to discuss strategies to end the racial discrimination that they deemed the ultimate barrier to educational parity.[50] Because of their vulnerability as public school teachers and a real fear of reprisals by whites, most members of the group shunned publicity. In a 1984 interview, Johnson recounted that most members of the group belonged to the NAACP and used its Louisville branch as a platform for public comments on civil rights issues. William H. Perry, a Louisville black school teacher opposed to the informal group, charged that it attempted to monopolize black educator demands for educational equality. He argued that it wielded undue influence over the educational progress of Louisville blacks.[51] Clearly, Cole and Johnson did not represent all black teachers in Louisville. Dr. George D. Wilson of Louisville Municipal, who served as the Kentucky Negro Education Association's research committee chairman, took the middle ground.[52] He argued that blacks were victims of Kentucky's persistent de facto and de jure racial discrimination in education, but instead of condemning those responsible, he appealed to school district superintendents' "spirit of justice and fair play" to first remove the racial differentials in salaries paid to black teachers.[53] School districts largely ignored this moderate 1938 KNEA request because of the mixed signals sent to whites regarding black educator acceptance of the segregated system and their unequal working conditions. If Wilson's comments were at all representative, Kentucky black teachers, while continuing to accept the existence of segregated schools, had become restive about their unequal salaries.

Another example of internal division among black educators occurred during the 1937-38 Kentucky State–West Kentucky Industrial merger controversy. Black advocates and opponents of the merger outlined their positions in the January-February 1939 issue of the *KNEA Journal,* with opponents outnumbering advocates. Whitney M. Young Sr. of Lincoln Institute and Atwood of Kentucky State defended the merger, while Albert E. Meyzeek of the Louisville Public Schools, William H. Fouse, president of the KNEA, Moneta J. Sleet of Paducah, and J. Bryant Cooper argued against it.[54] Such divergent views revealed that black educators failed to reach a consensus on the higher education that Kentucky blacks wanted. The

KNEA board of directors decided to poll the membership and study the issue more thoroughly.[55]

The 1938 merger compromise did not mean that black educators had moved to oppose racially segregated education. None of the statements by either side opposed segregation per se. Both sides had instead hinted that the best solution would be to improve higher education for blacks. That meant expanding existing institutions into comprehensive colleges truly equal to white ones that included both liberal arts and vocational programs. However, the merger arrangement arrived at by Chandler, Anderson, and others deftly skirted this issue.

Although Kentucky was thus left unpressured to consider the equality of education, it could not avoid the consequences of a Missouri case decided in the U.S. Supreme Court. In November 1938 the belief that educational segregation would continue indefinitely was shaken. Lloyd D. Gaines, a Missouri black college graduate, was denied admission to the University of Missouri law school because he was black. The denial of admission rested on two grounds: that Missouri law prohibited biracial classes and that a publicly supported jim crow law school existed at the black Lincoln University in Jefferson City, Missouri. After suing unsuccessfully in the federal courts, Gaines and his NAACP counsel appealed to the Supreme Court. It subsequently ruled that the state must provide separate but equal graduate and professional school opportunities to qualified blacks. In the 1938 ruling that affirmed segregation but demanded improved graduate education for blacks, it ordered the University of Missouri Law School to admit Gaines.[56]

This ruling required all states employing racially segregated education to reassess their graduate and professional offerings for blacks. Kentucky, which had decided only in March 1938 to create a truly comprehensive, public undergraduate college for blacks, now had to consider the even costlier project of providing state-supported graduate and professional education to blacks.

Black educator response to the *Gaines* decision came not from President Atwood or Dean Lane, but from W.H. Fouse, a high school principal and president of the KNEA, who wrote in the *Louisville Courier-Journal* that although blacks did not oppose separate education, "what the Negro does oppose and I believe rightly so, is unequal education." He also argued that if white Kentuckians wanted completely separate education, they should offer "absolute equality in educational opportunities" to the poorer blacks who could not afford to make up the difference between white and black schools.[57]

Within weeks of the *Gaines* decision and Fouse's comments, Governor Chandler decided not to decide. He convened a conference of black and white educators to investigate the implications of the *Gaines* ruling for Kentucky.[58] To permit blacks to attend the all-white graduate and professional schools at the University of Kentucky and the University of Louisville required an alteration in the 1904 Day Law, a move that Chandler firmly opposed.[59] Against the backdrop of that opposition, an interracial committee of college presidents and other educators met to propose the state's response to the *Gaines* ruling.

Complicating the committee's work was the necessity of completing the task before Chandler's administration expired and recently elected Keen Johnson's began. Chandler's appointment of the committee did not bind Johnson to abide by its recommendations. Under these constraints, the committee did not recommend significant changes in the educational system. The only committee meeting of substance, on 24 November 1939, produced publicity but little progress. Its preliminary report recognized the legal right of blacks to enroll in courses at the University of Kentucky *provided* that Kentucky State did not offer such courses and that the blacks involved refused to accept state aid for non-Kentucky higher education. The committee agreed that a subcommittee should investigate how many blacks might possibly enroll at the University of Kentucky professional and graduate schools. They also wanted information on the statutory changes necessary to permit desegregation. Rather than to confront an administration on its way out, the committee avoided making any substantive recommendations until the new governor and his administration assumed control.[60]

Sensing another victory deriving from its litigation against segregated higher education, the national NAACP declared that the 24 November 1939 report of the Kentucky committee was the "direct result of the campaign waged by the NAACP to open the doors of state universities in Southern and border states to all persons without regard to color."[61] As expected, the Kentucky legislature and the State Board of Education ignored the committee's findings. The general lack of support for the committee's recommendations among state legislators signaled to white college governance boards that it was unnecessary to make significant changes in Kentucky's segregated higher education system.[62]

In that climate it was inevitable that Governor Johnson also would avoid reform. Kentucky therefore followed the general practice of southern states that enforced segregation: to maintain or strengthen educational segregation unless a court order was issued. In an apparent effort to reinforce Kentucky's separate but equal policy, Kentucky State received provisional permission to offer graduate courses in agriculture and home economics during the 1939 and 1940 summer terms, but these course offerings ended when Kentucky State discovered that only the University of Kentucky had the legal authority to offer graduate degrees.[63] Since the courses did not lead to a degree, the college stopped offering them. Yet the state continued to claim that Kentucky blacks received an equal educational opportunity through the Kentucky State makeshift graduate program or through out-of-state tuition grants. A *Gaines*-style lawsuit would be seriously flawed because the state offered blacks so-called separate but equal undergraduate and graduate courses.

Although Kentucky refused to change its segregation law, Alfred Carroll, a graduate of Ohio's all-black Wilberforce University, attempted in February 1939 to enroll at the University of Kentucky. Representatives of the KNEA and the local NAACP met to devise a strategy to help him overcome Wilberforce University's unaccredited status and the Day Law prohibition. Charles Anderson, legal advisor to the Louisville NAACP, wrote Chief NAACP Counsel Charles Hamilton Houston in Washington that the university officials and the governor needed to work out "amicable arrangements" by notifying the attorney general of this case before the NAACP filed the test lawsuit.

Before these arrangements took shape, the university denied Carroll admission based on his unaccredited college degree and on the Day Law. The NAACP assistant special counsel, Thurgood Marshall, did not recommend litigation in this instance. He recommended instead that another, stronger test case on Kentucky segregation be initiated because the presence of Charles Anderson should give Kentucky blacks adequate legal counsel, and Marshall believed, according to a cryptic comment, "Kentucky is more or less civilized."[64] Marshall's benign vision of Kentucky changed in the next decade.

The Carroll case also forced President Atwood to clarify his position on the equalization of higher education opportunities. He wanted the parties involved to wait until the *Gaines* committee appointed by Governor Chandler had a chance to explore all the possibilities. Given strong white support for the Day Law, Atwood decided that a class-sharing arrangement between Louisville Municipal, Kentucky State, the University of Louisville, and the University of Kentucky was the best and perhaps most workable approach to equalize black higher education.[65]

In retrospect, the 1930-39 decade produced important changes in Kentucky black higher education. It lost one weak institution, Simmons University, and gained a strong replacement, Louisville Municipal College. State government centralized black higher education at Frankfort under Kentucky State and changed West Kentucky Industrial into a strictly vocational school. Kentucky black colleges established liberal arts curricula as did others in the southern and border states. Kentucky whites refused to amend the Day Law despite the *Murray* and *Gaines* Supreme Court rulings in 1935 and 1938, but those rulings nudged the Kentucky legislature toward providing graduate education to blacks. That meant giving $175 per term to blacks wanting graduate education if they enrolled in out-of-state universities,[66] a practice that kept blacks out of the state's graduate and professional institutions but conceded that selected blacks must be given an opportunity to enroll at non-Kentucky desegregated universities, most of which were nationally outstanding academic institutions.[67] The law that provided for the out-of-state education also undermined an original subtext of the Day Law—that blacks were distinctly inferior to whites and needed to be kept apart in order to maintain social order. Based on contemporary racial prejudice, white legislators, however, remained adamant in retaining the Day Law as originally written. Yet, educators of both races on the *Gaines* committee acknowledged the necessity of future, imprecise changes in the law. These changes required a redefinition of Kentucky higher education.[68] Until that fateful, distant moment, however, Kentucky black and white educators were required to operate a dual system of higher education.

In this dual system, most whites attended five state-supported colleges and twenty-five private colleges. Blacks attended one private and two public segregated institutions of uneven quality, if these schools had enough places for the state's black students. Quality higher education for blacks therefore depended on black administrators and faculty. Although Kentucky ranked consistently near the bottom among southern states in provision of funds for public higher education for blacks, Kentucky whites could argue that it was not the fault of whites if blacks failed to use the higher education opportunities provided to them. Based on statistical data (see the appendix), Kentucky's appropriations for black colleges and normal schools remained small but consistent for a declining black population in the first three decades of the twentieth century.[69] Again, it could be argued that the state should not be expected to provide more funds to educate fewer black collegians. Black educators were expected to manage their resources prudently and avoid any appearance of mismanagement of state funds, such as in the cases of Green P. Russell and Dennis H. Anderson. Later, President Atwood of Kentucky State and Dean Rufus Clement of Louisville Municipal did improve the image of black college administrators by using fiscal conservatism to make their institutions both academically credible and financially sound.

Further, black college presidents occasionally placed their own immediate needs ahead of those of the black community. Dennis H. Anderson's dictatorial control of West Kentucky Industrial contributed to its dissolution, to his dismissal, and to the transformation of the college into a vocational school. In another case, President Atwood's effort to centralize black higher education at Kentucky State produced opposition among key Kentucky black teachers and protective western Kentucky legislators. Although Atwood sought to improve higher education for all Kentucky blacks, the immediate result appeared to be more funding for the Frankfort college. Again, Kentucky black expectations for improved higher education were delayed by institutional defensiveness among the state's leading black educators.

4

Separate and Unequal, 1940-1948

THE 1938 BLACK COLLEGE merger, the turmoil over it, the battle for black leadership, and the *Gaines* Supreme Court ruling muddied the prospects of what all parties had hoped would be a stable education system, within the limits of Kentucky's depressed economy. Kentucky blacks wanting higher education were left with dubious choices. They attended Kentucky State or Louisville Municipal, both of which lacked the resources of white teachers colleges, or, upon completing undergraduate programs at these or at out-of-state colleges, they enrolled at out-of-state desegregated universities for graduate or professional training. The *Gaines* committee's final report, issued on 7 March 1940 after several meetings, recommended possible changes in the Day Law, but, failing to gain white political support, the report had little chance for real impact.

The prospect of amending the Day Law generated controversy between blacks and whites from 1940 to 1948. The debate over that alternative forced Kentucky white educators and politicians to bargain with blacks to ascertain what quality of segregated education blacks were willing to accept in lieu of changing the linchpin of school segregation. Black educators and activists responded by developing immediate strategies against segregation and for improved education. From 1940 to 1948 black educators and their few white allies crafted legal strategies to achieve a new goal of desegregated education—a goal that the *Gaines* ruling had already given birth to. The discomforting implications of the decision became readily apparent to Governor Chandler's committee of educators commissioned to analyze it.

The committee's conclusions reflected its racial division. White members, including the presidents of the University of Kentucky, the University of Louisville, and the four state teachers' colleges, agreed that the Day Law had not been overturned and that segregated higher education must continue. Conversely, the *Gaines* decision implied that whites should make improvements for black higher education. Black members of the committee, including the dean of Louisville Municipal and the president of the KNEA, sought for black colleges parity of funding with white institutions. Both factions in the committee accepted the premise that desegregated higher education was unlikely in the immediate future, but the black members wanted more than the out-of-state tuition law. They wanted black students to receive education funds equal to those provided to whites.

White educators on the committee refused to support such an extreme proposal; it would pose both financial and political problems for all public education. Only in 1934 had the state education department approved the minimum requirement of two years of college training for elementary school teachers, four years of college for secondary school teachers, and a master's degree for advanced, lifetime teaching certificates. Usually strapped for funds, school districts required their teachers to obtain additional teacher training. Fortunately, white Kentucky teachers had a variety of choices: a public university, a municipally supported private university, four public teachers' colleges, and twelve private four-year colleges. Black Kentucky teachers had only two four-year colleges, both of which offered general bachelor degrees in the arts and sciences and no graduate degrees.[1]

Compounding this inequity between white and black teacher preparation institutions were significant gaps in the basic literacy of Kentucky's citizens. If the U.S. Census of 1910's definition of illiteracy as an inability to write is accepted, 16.5 percent of all Kentuckians over ten years of age were illiterate. Although standing substantially better than the regional percentage of 23.1, the state remained substantially above the national percentage of 10.7. White regional illiteracy, however, was 12.8 percent compared to 40.1 percent among blacks. When Kentucky white illiteracy dropped eight percent during the 1920s and 1930s, black illiteracy remained twice the percentage of whites, 5 percent above the regional average and 4 percent above the national average. The declining population of Kentucky blacks, resulting from outmigration and declining birth rates, reduced the number of illiterates, but the remaining blacks made only minor gains in literacy compared to the improvement in white literacy during the period. Put simply, Kentucky was more literate than its southern neighbors but was not among the nation's intellectual elite.[2]

Since 1921 Kentuckians had, in a series of legislative investigations, scolded themselves on the poor quality of their schools. Following each report, the legislature and the people ignored the recommendations and failed to levy the necessary taxes to improve the educational system. One of those reports, that of the Kentucky Educational Commission of 1933, observed that "certain provisions of the Constitution pertaining to education, and many provisions of the school law, actually work as a deterrent to education efficiency." Kentucky historian Thomas Clark later said, "The constitutional mandate that the people every four years elect by popular vote a superintendent of public instruction has denied the Commonwealth the advantages of planning, promoting, and executing a progressive education program."[3] Each elected superintendent proposed perfunctory solutions—often politicized by the appointment of noneducators to positions associated with the task—for the improvement of the state's education system. With each new governor, Kentucky educators adjusted to a different paradigm for educational improvement and for reducing illiteracy. The result was superficial, inconsistent, and inefficient campaigns for expanding formal education for the state.[4]

Many Kentucky educators refused to be hindered by the educational politics. Kentucky's colleges became key institutions in moving the state's average education level beyond what nineteenth-century legislators called "a fair English education" of three elementary grades. In 1933 the legislature authorized the Kentucky Educational Commission to make recommendations for change in the state education system. The legislature's response to the commission's proposals was the 1934 revised Kentucky School Code, which, as already indicated, expanded the duration of higher education and the qualifications required for teachers and staff. Despite this attempt to provide better-prepared teachers, increasing the numbers of formally educated Kentuckians remained a Herculean task. One indicator of its enormity appeared in the 1940 census of Kentucky.

The census of 1940 did not reveal the actual literacy of its respondents. Instead, it recorded the highest grade completed by each respondent. Of the 1.4 million Kentuckians 25 years of age and older, 32.4 percent of whites had completed eight years of elementary school, compared to 18.8 percent for blacks. The largest group of educated blacks, 26.8 percent, had completed only one to four years of elementary school; 15.1 percent of whites fell into that category. At the college level, 6.8 percent of Kentuckians had finished one to three years of college. Of these, 4.4 percent were white, 2.1 percent were black, and .3 percent belonged to other races. Of the 4.7 percent of Kentuckians who had finished four years of college, 3.1 percent were white and 1.6 percent black. The median number of years of completed education for Kentucky blacks was 6.3 and for Kentucky whites 8.3. National levels were 5.7 years for blacks and 8.8 years for whites. Although blacks were statistically better off in Kentucky than in the nation at large, 83 percent of all blacks in the state had eight years or less of formal education, whereas only 72 percent of the whites were at that low a level of education. Clearly, more blacks than whites remained under-educated.[5]

Because the Day Law had prohibited interracial teacher education and had limited black teacher training, the need to increase the number of formally educated blacks grew larger. More black teachers were needed for the state's 120 county school districts, 2 black colleges, and 1 vocational school. In the period 1910-40 black teachers had left the expression of their views to KNEA officers such as Albert E. Meyzeek and R.B. Atwood, who set forth in the *KNEA Journal* and the black press the dire fiscal straits of black schools. In the 1940s Kentucky black teachers and their leaders expanded the attacks, arguing that segregation prevented any social fairness to the nation's black citizens. Their concern with the unfairness of segregation accelerated as Kentucky blacks continued to concentrate in the state's large and small cities. In 1900 35.2 percent of all blacks lived in the urban areas, and by 1940 54.6 percent lived there.[6] Over a fifteen-year span, Paducah and Louisville blacks used their political clout in the 1920, 1925, 1932, and 1935 elections to extract concessions from whites. Black successes in the political arena and legal challenges in lower education areas increased the interest of civil rights activists in the problems of black schools and colleges.

Salaries too had become a prime concern for black educators. In 1940 the NAACP successfully challenged in court the race-based salary discrimination of a Virginia school district. That precedent encouraged seven black Louisville teachers and five citizens to attack the unequal black and white salary scales of the city's school district. Calling itself the Education Equalization Committee and including members of the Louisville NAACP and the Louisville Urban League, the committee devised a simple strategy to pressure the Louisville city schools to equalize salaries. Their effort led to a legal attack on the unequal funding of local black schools.

Subsequently, black elementary school teacher Valla Dudley Abbington informally complained to the Louisville board of education that the average black teacher pay was $1,490, whereas that of the average white teacher was $1,750.[7] To develop her case against the school board, Abbington, with the committee's assistance, sought legal counsel. At that time attorney and state representative Charles Anderson served as the Louisville NAACP chief legal counsel, but the Equalization Committee had begun to express private dissatisfaction with Anderson's lack of success in gaining civil rights legislation. His only major victory had been the 1936 Anderson-Mayer State Aid Act, and it affected only Kentucky black college graduates seeking graduate or professional degrees. So when Anderson indicated that "he was too busy" to pursue the Equalization Committee's case and suggested that the committee use Louisville black attorney Prentice Thomas as its chief counsel, members of the committee were privately relieved.[8]

With Thomas serving as local NAACP counsel, and with Charles H. Houston and Thurgood Marshall representing the national NAACP legal committee, Abbington's petition went to the school board in late November 1940. Following the board's rejection of the petition, the NAACP lawyers filed a complaint for relief with the U.S. District Court at Louisville in December 1940. The suit claimed that the Fourteenth Amendment's "equal protection" clause had been violated.[9]

Shortly thereafter, the Equalization Committee stepped up its activities on this matter. Its support of the Abbington case seemed to grow stronger when three similar out-of-state cases were resolved in favor of black plaintiffs. Moreover, the *Louisville Courier-Journal* recognized the case's significance; it published three consecutive editorials in December 1940 supporting Abbington's stand.[10]

Confronted by such negative publicity, the Louisville board began to equivocate in the matter of race-based salary discrimination. Although the board said it would phase in the equalization of salaries, the NAACP legal counsel pressed on with the lawsuit.[11] In response, the Louisville board of aldermen under Mayor Joseph D. Scholtz undertook to divert other city revenues to make up the salary differences. Based on a lengthy letter sent to Mayor Scholtz on 21 December 1940 from John Miller, president of the board of education, the city and the board agreed to grant the black teachers their request.[12] The NAACP lawyers advised the Louisville black teachers to continue their suit until a consent decree had been won; the teachers, however, agreed with the court's dismissal of the case in October 1941 after they had signed contracts equal to those of whites.[13]

In the midst of organizing the case for the Louisville black school teachers, attorney Thomas directed Thurgood Marshall's attention to questions posed by two Berea College faculty members who were interested in challenging the Day Law by enrolling a black student from Appalachia. Interest in this approach developed from the college's mission, since it served only Appalachian students and not other Kentucky students. Ultimately, this tactic failed because Thomas did not have the funds to travel to the Appalachian region and find an interested student.[14] Despite the failure, Thomas's interest in opposing the Day Law revived when he heard that a black student had been secretly attending the all-white Southern Baptist Theological Seminary in Louisville.[15] This development encouraged Thomas to expand his anti–Day Law efforts.

On 18 June 1941, during the Abbington trial preparations, Thomas wrote Marshall, "[A] statewide committee has been formed to have a student apply at the University of Kentucky this fall."[16] The unidentified members of the Anti–Day Law Committee then rallied to support Kentucky black student William Harkins's attempt to enroll at the university. This test case failed ostensibly because Harkins did not have a college preparatory background strong enough to meet the university's academic requirements and because the committee prepared the case poorly.[17]

Undaunted, civil rights activists again targeted the Day Law. They focused their attention on the University of Kentucky graduate and professional schools, and it was decided that to desegregate these colleges a well-prepared black student had to seek admission to an academic program not offered at Kentucky State.

A volunteer, Charles Lamont Eubanks, expressed an interest in attending the University of Kentucky engineering school. Eubanks, an honors graduate of black Louisville Central High School, filed suit against the university after being denied admission based on race.[18] Pleaded by attorneys Charles H. Houston and Thurgood Marshall of the national NAACP office, Eubanks's case plodded through the Eastern Kentucky federal district court in Lexington from 1941 through 1945. Eubanks's legal team argued that the state neglected to provide separate but equal training for black engineering students.[19]

From the beginning, the suit met with frustrating political and judicial problems as well as opposition from state government. In November 1941 Gov. Keen Johnson requested the State Board of Education to authorize the opening of Kentucky State's "school of engineering" in September 1942. Composed of one teacher, two students, and meager engineering teaching materials, it became part of the state's effort to defeat Eubanks's suit by demonstrating that "equal facilities" existed.[20] The state also used delaying tactics to prevent the case from coming to trial as quickly as the plaintiff wanted. Eubanks's attorneys inadvertently contributed to this process by incorrect deliveries of summonses and errors in naming the defendants.[21] Eubanks also became the target of personal criticism by anonymous Louisville blacks who disliked his brashness in suing the university and creating potential race relations "trouble" between blacks and whites.[22] During this time Eubanks's marriage ended in divorce. The case was postponed, a development that for Eubanks meant further denial of his education and increased personal frustration.[23]

By 1944 Eubanks's case lost ground because the state's lawyers argued that a separate but equal engineering school existed in Frankfort at Kentucky State; the delay had given the state enough time to pressure the State Board of Education to strengthen Kentucky State's makeshift engineering program. The defendants also claimed that the prospect of Mr. Eubanks or anyone successfully completing an engineering program in wartime appeared unlikely.[24]

While Eubanks's attorneys sparred with the university counsel over his entry, there appeared another tactic directed at achieving black enrollment in the university. During the 1944 session of the legislature, Charles Anderson, who had declined to participate in both Abbington's and Eubanks's cases, offered a bill that would retain the Day Law's segregation provisions except in professional and graduate schools.[25] Anderson's legislative proposal would not destroy the Day Law but would establish a selective exception to its provisions.

The bill was opposed by rural Jessamine County white legislator James R. Dorman, who proposed a bill to increase appropriations for Kentucky State.[26] It would, he alleged, make the college the equivalent of the University of Kentucky.[27] The two bills reached the legislative docket on the same day. A motion to take up Dorman's bill failed. After approval by the rules committee, Anderson's bill received the support of an urban contingent of thirty-one Republicans and nine Democrats. Thirty-two Democrats and six Republicans from rural areas voted against the measure.[28]

The House struggle for Anderson's proposal evoked the opposition of black civil rights activist and publisher William Warley, executive committee member of the Louisville branch of the NAACP and publisher of the *Louisville News*. He urged support for the Dorman bill, saying, "[It] declares absolute equality of Kentucky State and the University of Kentucky and the University of Louisville. . . . If this bill should become law Kentucky State College would become a million dollar university giving to Colored youth law, medicine, and everything the 'white' universities would give and give it as went along in his schooling."[29]

Warley's public opposition manifested itself at a Louisville NAACP branch meeting at which he and executive committee member Stephen A. Burnley, in a rare show of black leader dissension, voted *not* to support Anderson's bill. Kentucky's largest NAACP branch, composed of black school teachers, ministers, social activists, and laborers, discussed both bills at length. Finally, the executive committee voted to support the bill, with twenty-three in favor and two—Warley and Burnley—against. The committee supported Anderson's bill because it would have forced the state to conform to the *Gaines* decision, an objective of the NAACP's national office. Even the potential beneficiary of Dorman's bill, President Atwood of Kentucky State, came out in support of Anderson's proposal, citing the need for true graduate facilities for Kentucky blacks.[30]

Warley opposed Anderson's bill because it allowed unequal education for most blacks, provided equal education for the tiny minority of Kentucky blacks who completed their bachelor's degrees, and would save the state treasury at least $1 million. Warley argued that whites would be forced to spend more on Kentucky State and black higher education generally if Dorman's bill passed.[31]

Warley's activism made him the only Kentucky black newspaper publisher supporting the Dorman Bill. Other black Louisville newspapers, the *Louisville Leader* and the *Louisville Defender,* lent their support to the Anderson bill. Despite Warley's opposition,

Louisville NAACP branch president Lyman T. Johnson wrote acting NAACP national executive secretary Roy Wilkins that the branch had decided to provide prudent support of a "Citizens Committee" promoting the Anderson bill.[32]

With the controversy surrounding the bill, the campaign to obtain for Kentucky blacks higher education equal to that provided whites came to a critical crossroads. Dorman's bill, although proposing financial increases for Kentucky State to make it appear equal to the university, had the potential of undermining any lawsuits by black students who claimed a denial of equal higher education at Kentucky's segregated public colleges. The state could claim that it offered, in good faith, separate but equal higher education facilities and programs. Meanwhile, endorsement of Anderson's bill by the *Louisville Courier Journal,* by the Civil Rights Committee of the predominantly black National Bar Association, by the ad hoc black Citizens Committee of Louisville, by the Kentucky NAACP branches, and by a majority of the Louisville NAACP branch sustained Anderson's belief that his approach was a practical method to weaken the Day Law. Warley's opposition, however, "gave some [people] rather cool to the bill a good excuse to oppose it on the grounds the Negro people themselves were divided on it."[33] Warley inadvertently gave segregation supporters ammunition for their cause, as had Meyzeek and Parrish in the 1920s.

The only glimmers of hope were the forty yes votes the House of Representatives gave Anderson's bill, a development demonstrating that the idea of total segregation outlined in the 1904 Day Law had lost its previous strong white legislator support.[34] It also suggested that white legislators preferred ending racial segregation in a small, selective part of the educational system rather than to equalize funding for all black higher education. As for the eventual fate of Anderson's bill, it became bottled up in the Senate rules committee and died on 15 March 1944.[35]

As the Warley-Anderson quarrel subsided in late 1944, the Eubanks case went on its slippery slope to oblivion. On 8 January 1945 a federal district judge, citing court rules, dismissed the case because the plaintiff had failed to prosecute it within two terms of the court.[36] Charles H. Houston and Thurgood Marshall believed that the case had insurmountable problems.[37] Eubanks, it appears, had become an incidental participant in a legal process completely foreign and confusing to him. He agreed to abide by his lawyers' advice to back off from the issue and abandon the lawsuit.[38]

Nonetheless, the commotion external to Eubanks's case affected Kentucky black higher education. Although the plaintiff's attorneys failed to argue adequately the original complaint, the University of Kentucky fought back with legal technicalities and the establishment of a jim crow engineering school. University trustees successfully avoided a direct confrontation over the validity of the Day Law, which the case originally sought to provoke. Defenders of racial segregation also took solace in that it remained unscathed by excluding Eubanks from the university. However, opponents of the Day Law had pushed the legislature to consider, ever so briefly, a dilution of the color line in graduate and professional education.

The debate surrounding the Anderson and Dorman bills and the failure of the Eubanks case revealed a persistent structural weakness within Kentucky's NAACP branches: they could not mount an effective campaign to overturn one law. This debacle was attributed to the lack of a state NAACP conference to attack statewide racial discrimination problems. Had there existed a state conference organization, Eubanks's attorneys would have had the support of all the Kentucky branches in their respective cities. A conference organization might also have reduced the logistical problems faced by the NAACP's Washington attorneys, who had to work both with the Louisville branch of the NAACP and the eastern Kentucky district of the federal district court, 110 miles east in Lexington. That experience, among others, persuaded the branches to establish a Kentucky conference in 1946.[39]

The dismissal of the Eubanks case also resurrected the intermittent public disagreement between Charles Anderson and Pres. R.B. Atwood over civil rights tactics. Anderson blamed the case's failure on Atwood, who he believed had created the makeshift engineering school that allowed defense attorneys to claim that "there was no denial or failure to provide equal education facilities within the state." Atwood did not respond immediately to Anderson's charges of collusion with the defenders of segregation. He did later accuse the black press of instigating these and other disputes. "After all," he wrote in 1964, "a fight between two prominent Negro leaders was news." To repair the rift between the two, *Louisville Defender* publisher Frank L. Stanley arranged for Atwood and Anderson to exchange views at a Louisville church meeting. This public forum resolved what Atwood considered an unfortunate misunderstanding.[40] Again, the state's black leaders had allowed their internal disagreements and personal disputes to divert attention from the legal campaign against segregation.

Although the Eubanks case faltered, the NAACP legal team of Thurgood Marshall, Charles H. Houston, Robert Carter, and Leon Ransom continued their attack on segregation with a successful 1944 U.S. Supreme Court decision invalidating Texas's all-white primary.[41] This decision created a significant precedent in opposition to racial segregation in local and state political primaries. Since Kentucky already permitted blacks to vote in primaries and general elections, the case had little impact on Kentucky except to encourage civil rights activists to continue antisegregation litigation.

Another indirect influence during this period was the admission of social scientists that racial segregation remained a nagging, unsolved American social problem. Swedish sociologist Gunnar Myrdal's compelling 1944 analytical compendium on American blacks, *An American Dilemma,* pointed out that the United States could not maintain the fraud that blacks enjoyed equal treatment in every aspect of life while they continued to have inferior housing, schools, jobs, and political rights. Myrdal also concluded that black higher education suffered from an intellectual blindness: white educators, already suspicious of the quality of black higher education, did not treat black colleges as equivalent to white institutions in the higher education system.[42] If blacks completed their education under segregation, their education was presumed inferior, thus keeping them in a subordinate, second-class status.

Those assumptions on the part of white educators came under attack during the post–World War Two era when American higher education experienced enrollment of older, nontraditional students. Returning World War Two veterans used the G.I. Bill benefits to enroll in college. As the upper-class and upper-middle-class students soon discovered, American colleges now admitted more low- and middle-income students, some of whom were black.[43] Confronted with war-tempered black veterans, who were unwilling to accept the pervasive color line in the academy, black higher education institutions strained to absorb them and endure the socio-economic changes wrought by four years of conflict. In the years immediately after World War Two all higher education underwent increased self-scrutiny—as did the nation—as it struggled to cope with both social change and demands for more education opportunities.

Consequently, internal studies of higher education, such as that of the 1947 National Commission on Higher Education, exposed the chronic weaknesses of all higher education, including the form and function of black colleges. In some instances these colleges continued as subterfuges for the maintenance of racial segregation; they received additional funding and were permitted to expand to provide temporary "equal" higher education opportunities for blacks. Although not specifically cited in the study, the Kentucky State "school of engineering," hastily organized in 1941, fit this category.

Kentucky, like other southern and border states, recognized that the opponents of segregation were no longer willing to accommodate the philosophy or practices of racial segregation. Although the white leadership claimed that Supreme Court precedents protected each state's racial segregation laws, the national political leadership felt otherwise.

In 1948 Pres. Harry Truman issued an executive order decreeing the elimination of racial segregation in the U.S. Armed forces.[44] With de jure segregation outlawed in the military, de jure civilian racial discrimination was weakened indirectly, and the prospect for future racial desegregation brightened.

In southern states individual blacks attacked segregation. When returning black veterans attempted to earn college degrees through the G.I. Bill of Rights and sought admission to white colleges and universities, southern state governments used every method to keep them and other blacks out. To defeat lawsuits alleging the denial of opportunities afforded whites, southern state governments continued the post-*Gaines* practice of creating ad hoc graduate and professional "schools" on state-supported black college campuses.

In 1946 black college students sued Louisiana State University as they tried to enroll in the law and medical schools. In response the state created an out-of-state tuition grant program. In 1947 the Louisiana state board of education permitted the establishment of a law school at all-black Southern University in Baton Rouge.[45] In a similar 1945 case in South Carolina, the state legislature authorized the single black state-supported college to create law and medical departments. After a July 1946 federal district court ruling that a black applicant must receive legal training in the state, the South Carolina legislature created a law school of three professors at South Carolina State College for Negroes.[46]

In Kentucky Gov. Simeon Willis first reacted by creating in 1945 an investigative body on Kentucky blacks. Willis ordered the Commission on Negro Affairs to "study all the facts and conditions relating to the economic, education, housing, health and other needs for the betterment of Negro citizens of Kentucky."[47] Black leaders Charles Anderson, Dr. Maurice F. Rabb of Louisville, and W.H. Perry Jr. from the KNEA led the interracial commission in analyzing the social and economic status of Kentucky blacks. Assisted by interracial advisory committees named by the commission, the group found that racial segregation hampered blacks in all areas of life except voting. The commission's final report made recommendations in the six areas of housing, welfare, education, economics, civil affairs, and health. The report's authors hoped it would help in the long term to mitigate the effects of racial discrimination. In its recommendations, the commission did not ask for the complete destruction of segregation but proposed carefully framed modifications that would permit blacks to exercise their rights and somehow cope with a racially segregated Kentucky. It was unclear from commission proceedings whether its black members agreed with these conclusions.

The commission's education subcommittee examined the segregated education provided to Kentucky blacks and found it unequal to that provided to whites. The subcommittee also recognized that blacks no longer accepted the poor quality and insufficient quantity of their education. Particularly egregious was the inequality existing at the level of higher education. For example, Kentucky State offered two degrees—bachelor of arts and bachelor of science—with fifteen majors. The University of Kentucky offered whites eleven undergraduate and professional degrees. In most of the degree programs students had a wide choice of majors within the divisions of the university.

The commission also ranked Kentucky below the neighboring states of Tennessee, Virginia, and West Virginia in 1945-46 annual state expenditures per black college student. Tennessee spent $500,000 for 1,000 students, or $500 per student, while Kentucky allocated $150,000 for 426 students, or $352 per student. West Virginia spent twice as much as Kentucky—$621,500 for 803 students—and Virginia appropriated more than three times as much—$1,196,740 for 1,121 students. Another state, Oklahoma, operated a segregated black college and had a black population ratio approximating Kentucky's 7.2 percent but spent more than twice as much—$373,000 for 460 students.[48] To summarize, the commissioners hoped fiscal disparities between black and white education would disappear when "Kentuckians allow[ed] their consciences and not their fear[s], to dictate public policies in education."[49]

In this context the commission admitted that Kentucky offered graduate education to the public with "the exception of the Negro people."[50] The report's authors sidestepped the question of that day's racial exclusion by saying that the issue must be "faced at some future time."[51] Until then, the commission said, Kentucky State should improve its undergraduate courses, and graduate courses at the University of Kentucky should be made "available without distinction of race," a proposal that implied an eventual black admission to the university.[52]

As had happened with the earlier *Gaines* Committee report, legislator indifference to the commission's report marginalized its significance, Charles Anderson, who was the sole black legislator in the General Assembly, did not have enough political clout to gain passage of the bills necessary to remove Kentucky's de jure color line. Moreover, the report's release on 1 November 1945, only a few days before the general election, limited the possibility that its conclusions would enter the political debate.

The report exposed continuing dissatisfaction with the dual system of higher education. In the editorial "Kentucky Must Make a Choice," the *Courier-Journal* argued that either white colleges must accept blacks or Kentucky must spend vast sums on the equalization of Kentucky State.[53] The dean of the University of Kentucky's graduate school also admitted that the choices had narrowed to two: "a dual system of professional and graduate schools at considerable more expense, or [the admission of] Negro students to existing courses."[54] No longer disagreeing as they had in the 1938 merger controversy and the Eubanks case, black leaders Charles Anderson and R.B. Atwood both supported the report's key education recommendations.[55]

In the midst of this debate, Gov. Simeon Willis appointed a black Republican and loyal supporter, Onis M. Travis of Lexington, to the State Board of Education.[56] Travis, a past member of the Republican State Central Committee, became the first black invited to enter the political structure at the state appointive level. Although his appointment was a political reward, it symbolized the accumulating social and political power of the board over black education. The board supervised all public elementary and secondary schools and, since 1938, Kentucky State and West Kentucky Vocational School. Travis's appointment also came when black votes had contributed significantly to the election of Republican Willis to the governorship.

Although Travis's moderation on race issues qualified him for such a visible political appointment, other blacks pressed for renewing the struggle against all racial discrimination laws and overt practices. Indeed, they experienced continual reminders of the strident and uncivil character of Kentucky's antiblack temperament. One such reminder occurred in August 1945 when three black WACS were beaten by a white mob in Elizabethtown, Kentucky, near Fort

Knox. After military authorities were summoned and arrested the black women, they were acquitted of violating military rules and quickly transferred from the area. The incident reminded Kentucky blacks that violent racists ignored both the rule of law and the state's alleged racial civility. Undeterred by such incidents, Kentucky black activists continued their legal and political attacks against racial segregation.[57]

Black activist Lyman T. Johnson taught at Louisville Central High School after earning a master's degree in history from the University of Michigan in 1933. With his preparation and experience, Johnson felt himself equipped for a role beyond that of high school history and government teacher. He joined the Louisville NAACP branch and the attack against Kentucky segregation laws and traditions.[58]

In his 1948-49 term as NAACP branch president, Johnson quietly sought another individual suitable for participation in a case that would again test the Day Law. An unnamed Louisville black woman agreed to apply at the University of Louisville in March 1948.[59] According to Johnson, she withdrew from the project after the *Louisville Defender* revealed that the NAACP had supported her enrollment. The untimely publicity and her withdrawal pressured the Louisville branch of the NAACP not to pursue the project as planned.

As the Louisville branch of the NAACP contemplated its next action against segregation, local black political leadership unexpectedly changed. In the fall of 1947, Charles Anderson abruptly declined to run for another term in the state legislature. His refusal apparently derived from the growing impatience of the Louisville black community and press and from their charges that the representative had failed in the 1944 and 1946 sessions to weaken the state's segregation laws.[60] Under such criticism, Anderson accepted an appointment as the first black assistant Commonwealth's Attorney (prosecutor) in Jefferson County, Kentucky.

In the 1947 primary election, voters in the forty-second House district turned to Dennis Henderson, a graduate of Howard University Law School and a partner in the Ray and Henderson Law Agency.

Following his election in November, he persuaded Charles Anderson to chair a local citizen advisory committee organized to propose anti-segregation bills. This action expanded community involvement in the antisegregation law campaign.[61]

In the same election Earle C. Clements became Kentucky's governor. Clements and Clarence L. Timberlake, black educator and president of West Kentucky Vocational School, had maintained a long and cordial relationship, and, although Timberlake's influence on Clements cannot be measured, Timberlake intimated that Clements's "moderate" racial views resulted from their long friendship.[62] Even so, Clements did not move quickly to end racial discrimination. Timberlake's covert attempt to persuade Clements to end segregation was not immediately successful.

Instead, Clements was governed by his conviction that most Kentucky whites, notwithstanding the *Gaines* decision and the 1945 Commission on Negro Affairs recommendations, remained firmly and publicly opposed to desegregation of all schools, public accommodations, and housing. Clements, who later claimed that he privately supported school desegregation, acquiesced in the conventional white view that de jure racial segregation should not be ended immediately. Ultimately, he did respond to the desegregation tide when national litigation forced all Kentucky white politicians to accede to important changes in the Day Law that led to its dissolution. Yet, black and white Kentucky politicians refused to address head-on that Supreme Court-approved foundation of Kentucky's racially segregated schools and colleges. Clements changed his public position, as did others, when court rulings mandated a softening of the color line. Racial segregation in education was a product born of law and sustained by the social accommodation by blacks and whites; its demise arrived via the same paths.

5

Desegregated but Still Separate, 1949-1954

THROUGH 1947 THE STRUGGLE of Kentucky blacks to achieve truly equal higher education had been stalemated by legal and legislative counter-measures. Litigation to remove race as a basis of admission to the University of Kentucky ended in defeat. Attempts by civil rights activists to repeal the Day Law itself failed as confusion among their ranks developed and unity among their opponents prevailed.

In 1948 approaches to breaking this deadlock seemed to promise frustration again to blacks. If they did nothing, they appeared to support segregated education. If they again fought segregation laws through the courts, another volunteer test case would be needed; and that volunteer's education might be delayed in the renewed effort to reach a distant and uncertain legal victory. In the interim, whites could either pressure the individual to abandon the lawsuit or erect new segregated facilities. To surmount these barriers, blacks might make another direct attempt to repeal the Day Law. Each choice, in its own way, centered on desegregating Kentucky education. If any one plan succeeded in making desegregated education a reality, other areas of society could be pressured to make similar transformations.

Some courageous blacks, with covert white support, fought school segregation in their own ways. In the eastern Kentucky town of Lynch, black educator John V. Coleman headed an integrated high school of ten black and fifteen white teachers during the last decade of the Day Law. Although it is not clear why the school district was willing to violate the Day Law, it may have been that the obvious financial saving to poor white and black taxpayers by operating a single high school made the risk worthwhile. In another case, Berea blacks used white school facilities by sneaking in when someone—a friendly staff member—turned off the lights. Once inside, blacks participated in classes or other activities. Mindful of the potential prosecution of both the school district and the college, the participants avoided publicizing these practices.[1]

While some Kentucky blacks and whites resisted the law directly, subtle changes in the demography of Kentucky black communities added momentum for change. Since 1930 Kentucky blacks had been moving away from rural areas and establishing stronger urban communities. In the 1940 census, seven of thirteen Kentucky communities of more than 10,000 persons had black communities of 10 percent or more. Louisville had 47,210 blacks in a total population of 319,077.[2] The presence of growing black communities pressured local and state governments to provide both more and better schools for Kentucky blacks. Black voters continued the established tradition of voting for candidates who supported their educational concerns. With the appointment of blacks Onis M. Travis to the State Board of Education and Clarence L. Timberlake to the Kentucky Textbook Commission, state politicians made overt but measured gestures to black voters for educational reform. This was also true for governors Simeon Willis and Earle Clements, who named blacks to state regulatory boards. Although Kentucky whites remained in the majority, these appointments put black educators in key positions to articulate and implement black community demands for truly equal education.

As a result of these appointments, the state legislature was challenged by Louisville's black community to end racial segregation. It took advantage of its sizable professional class of teachers, politicians, and attorneys to coordinate a new attack on the Day Law. Marshaling its resources and drawing on other experiences in fighting segregation and racial discrimination, the Louisville black community encouraged its state representative Dennis Henderson to file three bills in the 1948 regular legislative session addressing civil rights for blacks. The first bill established exceptions in the Day Law to permit blacks to attend white graduate and professional schools. The second allowed black nurses to take their training with white nurses at hospitals whose governing boards approved. The third and perhaps most unusual allowed blacks to try on clothing in department stores without being required to buy all the clothes tried on.[3]

The graduate school exemption and the department store bill were rejected by the legislature because they produced immediate changes in racial practices. The narrowly defined and less-threatening nursing school bill, however, passed. For the first time since 1904, limited biracial education was legal in Kentucky. Because the law shifted the burden of introducing desegregated education to hospital governing boards, white legislators passed legislation that allowed Kentucky blacks to receive medical education in the private, white nursing schools and not at public expense or under public control. This provision removed the ultimate responsibility for desegregation from the legislature and Governor Clements, who did not veto the bill and later took credit for its passage.[4]

As the statute took effect, desegregation efforts elsewhere created discomfort within other prosegregation state governments. An Oklahoma case centered on the fight of Ada Lois Sipuel Fisher to gain admission to the University of Oklahoma Law School. Ignoring her academic credentials, the university barred her on the basis of race.[5] Her attorneys then petitioned the Oklahoma Supreme Court to require the law school to admit her. When that body rejected her petition because she had failed to ask for separate but equal legal training, her lawyers appealed the case to the U.S. Supreme Court.

Using social science data, findings of the President's Commission on Higher Education, and studies completed by Gunnar Myrdal and others, the Supreme Court ruled that Fisher's legal education was to begin immediately. Following announcement of the decision on 12 January 1948, Fisher requested immediate admission to the law school during its winter term beginning 29 January. At this point the Oklahoma legislature intervened to establish a separate black law school in the state capital's law library through the governing board of black Langston University. Undaunted, Fisher's attorneys pointed to the obvious academic deficiencies of the "Langston University Law School" and called the legislature's action contrary to the Supreme Court order.[6]

The NAACP lawyers then argued that inferior education provided under segregation had become the central issue.[7] Fisher therefore had not received immediate admission to a superior law school at the University of Oklahoma as suggested by the U.S. Supreme Court. Equivocation and legal subterfuge nominally provided her with "equality of educational opportunity," but it was hardly equal to that afforded whites.[8]

As Fisher and her attorneys struggled against Oklahoma's defenses of segregation, governors of nine southern states—including Kentucky—agreed to prevent similar cases by developing a higher education consortium called the Southern Regional Compact. It would permit member states to provide joint separate but equal graduate and professional facilities for blacks while keeping existing state universities for whites only. The compact's initial project focused on the purchase, with federal funds, of the financially strapped Meharry Medical College in Nashville, Tennessee, for use as a regional black medical school. Meharry, a privately operated black medical school since 1879, had incurred such heavy debts that some external support had become necessary for it to remain open.[9] Kentucky participated in the planning conference for the compact. Lt. Gov. Lawrence Wetherby attended and concurred in the majority's plans to maintain racial segregation with the aid of federal funds.[10]

The board of education of the Methodist Episcopal Church (South), which had originally established Meharry but no longer provided direct financial support, opposed this plan because it would create a separate educational system for blacks in medical education—an area of constant failure in southern higher education systems. Nashville black leaders and black newspaper editors across the country also criticized the proposal for the same reason.[11] Kentucky blacks would be immediately affected because of the 1948 law that permitted biracial nursing education.

Above left, Clarence Timberlake, president of West Kentucky Vocational School for Colored Persons (Timberlake Papers, Forrest G. Pogue Special Collections, Murray State University Archives). *Above right*, John H. Jackson, president of State Normal School for Colored Persons from 1886 to 1898 and Kentucky Normal and Industrial Institute for Colored Persons from 1907 to 1910 (photo from the *Kentucky Headlight;* courtesy of Kentucky Historical Society). *Below*, Normal School students with Professor Paul William Lawless Jones (standing, right) in 1913 (photo by Gretter Studio, Frankfort; courtesy of Kentucky Historical Society)

Above, the instructional buildings on the main campus of the Normal School in 1916 (photo by Gretter; courtesy of Kentucky Historical Society). *Below*, President Rufus B. Atwood with 1931 Kentucky State College graduates (photo by Cusick; courtesy of Kentucky Historical Society)

Above, Kentucky State Industrial College Orchestra in 1931 (photo by Cusick; courtesy of Kentucky Historical Society). *Below*, domestic science class at the Normal School, circa 1900-1906 (photo by Gretter; courtesy of Kentucky Historical Society)

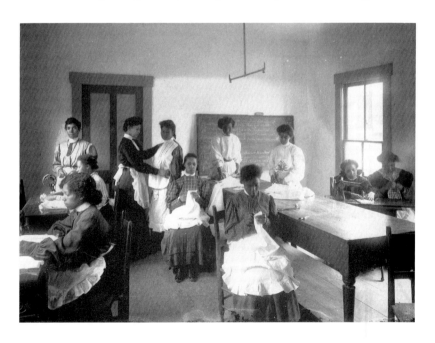

Above, the first graduating class of Kentucky State Normal School for Colored Persons, 1890 (courtesy of Kentucky State University–Blazer Library Photographic Archives). *Left*, William J. Simmons, president of State University and founder of Eckstein Norton Institute, 1888 (from Simmons Bible College Records, University of Louisville Archives). *Below*, Panoramic view of Kentucky State Normal School main campus, circa 1910 (courtesy of Kentucky State University–Blazer Library Photographic Archives)

Above left, Dr. Martin Luther King Jr. and President Rufus B. Atwood in 1957 at the Kentucky State College Commencement. *Above right*, Green Pinckney Russell, president of Kentucky Normal and Industrial Institute, 1914-1923 and 1924-1929 (both courtesy of Kentucky State University–Blazer Library Photographic Archives). *Below*, President Charles Parrish (standing at right) in front of State University's Citizen's National Hospital, 1525 Jefferson Street in Louisville (from Simmons Bible College Records, University of Louisville Archives)

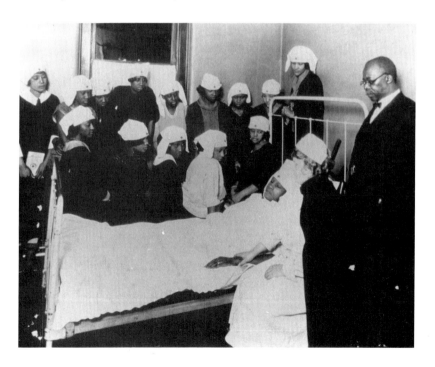

Above left, Lyman T. Johnson. *Above right*, Dr. Rufus E. Clement, dean of Louisville Municipal College, 1931-1936 (both from Louisville Municipal College Files, University of Louisville Archives). *Below*, President Charles H. Parrish (center front row) with Simmons University graduating class, year unknown (from Simmons Bible College Records, University of Louisville Archives)

Above, President Charles Parrish (second row center) with Simmons University Band, year unknown (Simmons Bible College Records, University of Louisville). *Below*, Louisville Municipal College library, 1937, with librarian Hortense H. Young in the background (Louisville Municipal College Files, University of Louisville Archives)

Above, Steward Hall, Simmons University and Louisville Municipal College, 1973 (photo by the author). *Below*, a wide-angle view of Artelia Anderson Hall, West Kentucky Industrial College, 1983 (photo by Richard Holland; courtesy of Kentucky Heritage Council)

On 19 May 1948 the U.S. Senate rejected a bill funding the compact and the purchase of Meharry Medical College.[12] This defeat encouraged blacks to renew their attack on the Day Law.

Since the 1945 failure of the Eubanks case, the only attack on the Day Law had been the Louisville NAACP's attempt to enroll a black graduate student at the University of Louisville. As indicated earlier, this endeavor failed after the student's name appeared in the *Louisville Defender* and such unwelcome publicity dissuaded her from the attempt to enroll.[13]

According to Lyman Johnson, the branch could not find another candidate who had both sufficient academic preparation and intellectual fortitude to challenge the law. When the membership asked Johnson, as branch president, to undertake the challenge himself, after some hesitation he agreed.[14]

Johnson made formal application to the doctoral program in history at the University of Kentucky.[15] After he had submitted the proper application forms and transcripts, the university registrar informed him, "Our policy is pretty well defined. We are prohibited by both State law and the State constitution from accepting the registration of a Negro."[16] On appeal to the university's trustees, Johnson was again denied admission. Local lawyers hired by the Louisville NAACP sought relief for Johnson in the federal district court at Lexington. Like the earlier desegregation efforts, Johnson's attempt forced the university administration and the Kentucky attorney general's office to act in concert to resist desegregation. The defendants were compelled to address the issue of graduate and professional education for blacks, as the 1939 Gaines Commission and the 1945 Commission on Negro Affairs had predicted. Although out-of-state tuition grants provided nominal educational opportunities to Kentucky blacks, they plainly violated the intent of the *Gaines* decision. After the filing of Johnson's suit, the university trustees asked the State Board of Education, which also served as the governing board of Kentucky State, to establish through the university another separate but equal graduate program on the Kentucky State campus.[17]

Although Gov. Earle Clements privately expressed his doubts about this project, Atty. Gen. Arvin E. Funk, University of Kentucky president Herman L. Donovan, and most State Board of Education members promoted it as a workable solution to the problem of providing black graduate education without violating the Day Law.[18] Again, Kentucky followed other southern states that had begun to devote significant funds to the creation of jim crow graduate programs.[19]

Unlike the 1939-40 graduate courses at Kentucky State, the 1948 graduate offerings operated under joint Kentucky State-University of Kentucky administrative control and could lead to a graduate degree. To carry out the plan, President Donovan of the university and the State Board of Education signed an agreement on 13 July 1948 to create a joint Kentucky State–University of Kentucky graduate program. The program required black graduate students to enroll at Kentucky State and to take their classes separately from white University of Kentucky students or in special sessions on the Kentucky State campus. Pressured by its advocates to supply funds for the venture, Governor Clements released forty-five thousand dollars from the Governor's Emergency Fund. With this funding, Attorney General Funk proclaimed that the plan would eventually develop "the best colored university in the nation."[20]

Funk's optimism notwithstanding, Kentucky black leaders remained skeptical. Albert E. Meyzeek, successor to O.M. Travis and the second black on the State Board of Education, publicly denounced the plan as "fantastic and unworkable" and voted against it.[21] In September 1948 Meyzeek contended that any advanced degree from Kentucky State under this plan would be a "joke" and he urged that black school principals not hire anyone with such a credential.[22] Lyman T. Johnson, whose attempted enrollment and lawsuit had pressured state agencies to enact the Kentucky State–University of Kentucky program, claimed that the state deliberately lied when it claimed that the plan provided separate but equal facilities.[23]

In reality, Kentucky's provision of black higher education was not equal, nor even adequate. White students consistently had more educational opportunities. At this time they could choose among five publicly supported colleges and fifteen private colleges, whereas blacks attended one public and one municipal college, neither one providing graduate degrees. Although the state appropriations per student at Kentucky State in 1949-50 were higher than at the state university—due in part to the Kentucky State–University of Kentucky program—blacks were still denied complete in-state graduate and professional degree programs.[24]

This statutory exclusion of blacks from better-equipped white colleges also forced the Kentucky State administration to deny admission to whites on the basis of race. In a peculiar 1948 incident, President Atwood refused admission to the college's first white applicant on the grounds that a white student, under Kentucky's Day Law, could not be educated with black students. In this instance Atwood concluded that racial segregation under the Day Law must apply to whites and blacks alike.[25]

While Kentucky struggled with the Johnson suit and its makeshift graduate program for blacks, another lawsuit, one similar to that of Ada Sipuel Fisher's, attracted national interest. Heman Marion Sweatt sued the Board of Regents of the University of Texas Law School because he had been refused admission to it. Sweatt's suit traveled a path similar to Johnson's. Sweatt's argument too focused on the denial of due process as guaranteed under the Fourteenth Amendment. His attorneys argued that limiting him to attendance at a hastily established three-room law school in Houston under Prairie View Agricultural and Mechanical College for Negroes would violate his constitutional right to equal treatment under the law. Sweatt contended that the black law school was certainly not the equivalent of the white University of Texas Law School. After he lost his suit in the Texas courts, he appealed to the U.S. Supreme Court.[26]

Meanwhile, Lyman Johnson's attorneys pursued his case at the federal district court level in Kentucky while the Louisville branch and the state conference of the NAACP solicited funds and public support for his legal expenses.[27] The campaign for funds followed internal disputes between the Louisville NAACP branch, the state conference, and national office lawyers concerning which case to support. Walter White, executive secretary of the NAACP, agreed with Johnson that the bickering had to stop.[28]

Although blacks finally presented a united public stand on Johnson's case, the Louisville branch also experienced internal conflict over legal personnel. Robert Carter, NAACP assistant special counsel, wrote in his personal notes on 23 February 1949 that James Crumlin and Alfred Carroll, both of whom had participated in the early stages of the case, "seemed very much embittered because they were afraid that the case would be taken out of their hands."[29] Their bitterness came in the wake of the procedural mistakes made by the national office legal team several years earlier in the Eubanks case. Also, removal of the case from their hands would suggest incompetence. In any event, this was a case that the black community would watch closely and that Crumlin and Carroll both had wanted.

Carter also had to contend with the suspicions of the Louisville branch that the national NAACP intended to delay or forgo Johnson's appeal in favor of the Fisher and Sweatt cases, which covered the same ground.[30] Carter convinced the Louisville branch's legal redress committee during a February 1949 visit that the national NAACP would support the Johnson case if the branch membership allocated at least five thousand dollars, which was needed to defray appeals costs. Lyman Johnson argued that Carter wanted the branch to support the Fisher and Sweatt cases only.[31] After Carter left the meeting, the Louisville branch membership voted to support the Johnson litigation with or without national NAACP support. Its first step was the formal appointment of James Crumlin as the local attorney in charge.[32]

Soon the Louisville Association of Teachers in Colored Schools and the KNEA voted to collect thirteen hundred of the five thousand dollars needed for the prosecution of the case.[33] Johnson reported other contributions from the local community, and the *Louisville Defender* began to publish weekly tallies of funds raised.[34] Given this financial support, NAACP attorneys Thurgood Marshall and Robert Carter agreed to pursue the case, and the legal team of Marshall, Crumlin, and Carter began to develop its strategies and arguments.

The most crucial argument focused on the "equivalent" graduate courses offered on the Kentucky State campus by University of Kentucky faculty. Although many black graduate students were given the out-of-state tuition grants, Robert Carter found only four who had been permitted to use the Kentucky State–University of Kentucky graduate school arrangement. Low black participation showed that blacks had suspicions about the motives behind the Kentucky State–University of Kentucky graduate program.[35]

Their doubts were confirmed when black graduate students who had accepted out-of-state tuition grants were required to sign waivers affirming that they had declined to attend Kentucky's "separate but equal" graduate school, therefore strengthening the state's legal position should these students decide to sue. On 5 April 1949 Robert Carter advised them not to sign the waiver and, if they were denied additional state grants, to present themselves for enrollment at the university in the next term.[36] The NAACP's advice was a part of the tactic by which blacks would "flood" white colleges. Advocated by James Nabrit, dean of Howard University Law School, that strategy was the same one employed against segregation in other southern states.[37]

The experiences of black graduate and professional students who participated in this plan fulfilled Meyzeek's original prediction of the plan's unworkability. The first law school student under the plan, John Wesley Hatch, suffered a difficult first semester. Initially, the University of Kentucky had hired eight law professors to teach black law students at Kentucky State. However, the professors themselves agreed to teach such students at the State Law Library in the state capitol, two miles from the campus. Given the absence of public transit for blacks, transportation to classes was difficult for Hatch. As he struggled to meet the standards of a first-year law curriculum, Hatch's legal studies became controversial when the eight faculty members resigned in protest, claiming that the jim crow law school threatened the accreditation of the university's white law school.[38] To replace them, the university hired four Frankfort attorneys. Hatch thus had to adjust to new teachers with four weeks left in the term.[39] President Atwood objected to the hirings because the original contract required regular University of Kentucky faculty.[40] Nevertheless, the university, the State Board of Education, and the attorney general's office maintained that they provided a separate but equal graduate education for blacks as required by the Supreme Court.[41]

The Hatch controversy did not impede the Johnson case. On 20 October 1948 the thrust of the Johnson case became more precise.[42] Johnson, as plaintiff, had to prove that Kentucky did not provide equal educational opportunity for a black person interested in completing a Ph.D. in history within the state.[43]

The University of Kentucky and the State Board of Education had failed to duplicate the university's graduate school programs, as they had the law school program, for blacks. The joint graduate school programs of Kentucky State and the University of Kentucky enrolled only eleven students from 1948 to 1950.[44] Unable to deny sparse enrollments and a paucity of funding for graduate courses, the university failed to prove that its graduate program offered equivalent educational opportunities for blacks. Depositions by University of Kentucky history professor Thomas Clark and university registrar Maurice Seay provided powerful evidence of the meagerness of the university offerings for blacks.[45]

Significantly, Johnson's attorneys had prepared one and one-half days of testimony from expert witnesses, including professors John Hope Franklin of Howard University and Goodwin Watson of Columbia University, to sustain the plaintiff's contentions.[46] But the commonwealth's own defense witnesses provided sufficient evidence for the plaintiff's case so that Johnson's attorneys rested their case and moved for summary judgment for the plaintiff.[47]

Shortly thereafter, on 30 March 1949, Judge H. Church Ford ruled in favor of plaintiff Johnson. Ford concluded that Johnson had not received an equal education opportunity and had been denied due process under the Fourteenth Amendment. His ruling, however, did not nullify the Day Law. If or when the state of Kentucky created a black graduate school equal to the one at the University of Kentucky, blacks would be required to seek initial admission at such a school. Until then, the University of Kentucky graduate school must admit qualified black applicants.[48]

Johnson's legal victory might have been transitory at best. The University of Kentucky board of trustees voted to appeal the decision to the U.S. Supreme Court, which was headed by a Kentucky-born chief justice, Fred Moore Vinson.[49] One trustee, Judge Edward C. O'Rear, demanded that Gov. Earle Clements convene a special session of the legislature to appropriate funds for the establishment of a black university equal to the University of Kentucky. O'Rear's passionate oratory almost led to a physical confrontation with Clements, who had not opposed the university's desegregation.[50]

Another trustee, Judge Richard Stoll, originally an opponent of black admissions at the university, sensed the dangerous volatility of the issue and persuaded other trustees to vote again. Given the explosive nature of this challenge to the university's policy, they reconsidered and decided not to appeal the ruling.[51]

The trustees' acceptance of black enrollments signaled the end of segregated higher education in Kentucky. Although some scholars suggest that the Johnson case had minor influence on the dissolution of southern school segregation, the case powerfully affected Kentucky.[52] It produced immediate results: blacks enrolled at the University of Kentucky. Atty. Gen. Arvin E. Funk and University of Kentucky president Herman L. Donovan no longer used the separate but equal argument to exclude black graduate students, and blacks began to undermine the racist premises underlying the Day Law by sharing education with whites in the best-equipped public college in the state.

The Johnson victory also exposed as a falsehood "equal higher educational opportunity" in Kentucky. Within segregated Kentucky higher education, qualified whites could live in the state and at moderate cost complete all requirements for both undergraduate and graduate degrees. Equally qualified blacks had to go elsewhere to establish residency in a state that did not subsidize black nonresident tuition and board. If these black students could acquire most of the tuition, board, and other fees, the state of Kentucky would provide three hundred dollars per black graduate student per year with the notion that this was somehow equivalent to the support provided Kentucky whites. Ironically, most of the institutions attended by the Kentucky black graduate students had better academic facilities, programs, and reputations than those available in the state to Kentucky whites.[53]

A section of the judge's decision declared that Kentucky's blacks and whites would receive the same level of graduate education only if the state built an all-black university equivalent to the University of Kentucky. This idea received no support from Governor Clements, his successors, or the state legislature. The only alternative, then, was to permit blacks to enroll for graduate education at the University of Kentucky.[54]

The Johnson victory also laid the groundwork for a later Paducah case that nearly overturned the Day Law. Joseph S. Freeland, a white Paducah NAACP attorney, wrote Thurgood Marshall in August 1949 requesting a copy of the original complaint filed by Johnson's attorneys against the university. Freeland's request came after the Paducah branch of the NAACP authorized him "to prepare suit against the [Paducah Junior College] authorities on behalf of a negro student who desires to attend the institution."[55] The Paducah Junior College case became especially important as Kentucky blacks continued to pressure Kentucky to end its racial segregation.

The Johnson case and the attendant makeshift graduate school at Kentucky State also induced some Kentucky whites to make public their views on desegregation. Harry Best, professor of sociology at the University of Kentucky, wrote to the *New York Times* on 2 September 1948 advocating repeal of the Day Law and urging black admissions to the university. In a contradictory statement, he claimed that his proposal would not violate the Day Law. He also believed blacks should be less insistent in demanding admission to white colleges and universities. Blacks should pursue desegregation

only at those institutions willing to desegregate.[56] Best's contradictory proposals, although moving at least some distance from the intransigence of segregation defenders, elicited little support from
whites and even less from blacks.

With white schools declining to voluntarily desegregate,
Louisville's black leadership conferred with University of Louisville
officials. A committee that included black leaders Albert E. Meyzeek
and I. Willis Cole met with white University of Louisville trustee
Fred H. Willkie and Pres. John W. Taylor in September 1948. The
meeting concerned black higher education and other matters "pertaining to the advancement of the race in these parts."[57] Although no
immediate changes in University of Louisville policies resulted, the
successful prosecution of the Johnson case generated an aggressive-
ness in the Louisville NAACP and the black professional class.[58] The
same black leadership, while supporting black candidates for the city
board of education, also fought to desegregate city parks, housing,
public accommodations, and libraries.[59]

After Johnson and the NAACP celebrated their victory, the
effort to realize its benefits became the next crucial step. Thirty-one
blacks enrolled in the University of Kentucky graduate school in the
1949 summer term were confronted with on-campus racial discrimination, including separate dining and library arrangements. Asst.
Atty. Gen. Marvin B. Holifield announced that the federal court
ruling permitting Johnson and other blacks to attend the university
did not invalidate the section of the Day Law requiring separate
classroom instruction.[60] Responding to this threat of segregation's
social reimposition, Johnson and his fellow students refused to use
the separate dining areas. Subsequently, seventeen crosses were
burned on the campus during the summer term as traditional reminders of white racist displeasure at the black presence; only one
of the burnings received any publicity.[61] Despite this intimidation
and questioning of Lyman Johnson afterward by the Federal Bureau
of Investigation, the small band of black graduate students attended
their classes and the term ended quietly; black matriculation at the
University of Kentucky had been achieved.[62]

With the success of the University of Kentucky case still fresh, Louisville black leaders and the NAACP branch set out to desegregate (among other facilities) their original target, the University of Louisville. The university president, John W. Taylor, argued in May 1949 that until there was a reversal of the 1908 *Berea* decision, the university must refuse black applicants.[63]

Debating this public posture internally, University of Louisville trustees struggled to determine their own position on the desegregation question. Confronted with a possible lawsuit against the university similar to that of Lyman Johnson's, the trustees had three choices. They could desegregate, they could resist desegregation using the Day Law as a rationale, or they could delay until the white community's reactions crystallized.[64] Finally, the university opted to delay desegregation pending resolution of the legal questions. One University of Louisville trustee, Wilson Wyatt, argued that the university, as a private institution, should admit blacks despite the Day Law. His motion was defeated.[65] Instead, trustees approved Rogers Morton's proposal that the university publicly endorse desegregation, exclude blacks per the Day Law, and invite a test case. Such a case did not occur, however, because the university failed to cite race as a reason for rejecting a black student.[66] Simultaneously, Louisville NAACP activists and University of Louisville trustees discussed changes in the Day Law that could be proposed to the 1950 session of the General Assembly.[67]

Meanwhile, University of Louisville faculty began to urge the trustees to drop their reliance on the Day Law as the basis for excluding blacks. After six meetings and the submission of a petition supporting black enrollments, signed by forty-five of the three hundred University of Louisville faculty, the trustees still refused to admit blacks, claiming that the legal questions remained unresolved.[68] In response, a committee of Louisville black leaders decided not to sue the university but to go themselves to the trustees and, according to Lyman Johnson, "see if a friendly adjustment of the situation could be worked out."[69] Johnson later maintained that he had orally threatened the trustees with a legal battle if they did not consider a desegregation plan.[70] Given five weeks by Johnson and the black committee to study the issue, the trustees announced that the university would "voluntarily desegregate" graduate schools in the 1950-51 academic year and undergraduate programs in 1951-52.[71]

Meanwhile, several southern states had created new arrangements for token black admissions to all-white state universities. For example, the University of Arkansas, which had permitted a black student to enroll in January 1948, admitted blacks to its graduate and professional school programs starting in the fall 1948 term.[72] Texas, embroiled in litigation by Heman Marion Sweatt, allowed blacks to attend the University of Texas if graduate programs could not be organized at the Texas State University for Negroes at Houston.[73] The state of Florida, entangled in litigation with five black graduate students, permitted black enrollments at the University of Florida until establishment of programs in law, pharmacy, and engineering at Florida Agricultural and Mechanical College for Negroes.[74]

In Kentucky, Gov. Earle Clements, who indirectly supported Dennis Henderson's 1948 law permitting an exception to the Day Law, did not oppose legislative efforts to introduce additional exceptions.[75] Other white leaders also began to look on desegregation more favorably. Among them were Barry Bingham, liberal Democratic publisher of the *Louisville Courier-Journal,* and James Hanratty, majority floor leader of the Kentucky House of Representatives. All, however, expressed only the most cautious, qualified support for future desegregation of Kentucky colleges.[76]

Blacks who held leadership positions occasionally attacked white officials who continued to use the Day Law to uphold segregated education. Among these black critics were Albert E. Meyzeek, who voted against the Kentucky State–University of Kentucky shared graduate school plan; James Crumlin, NAACP Louisville branch vice president and civil rights attorney; and even R.B. Atwood, who eventually criticized the graduate school arrangement linking the University of Kentucky and Kentucky State. Their criticisms were often provoked by white attempts to defend segregation as a "southern tradition" to the neglect of the rule of law. Given this black censure, the strong black community support of the Johnson case, and the mounting wave of litigation in other states, Kentucky white civic and political leaders who had formerly supported segregated schools began to revise their positions toward desegregation, including modification or repeal of the Day Law.[77]

A sign of these changing attitudes appeared during meetings of the Committee for Kentucky. Organized in 1943 by diverse statewide labor, farming, and urban organizations, it served as a private, interracial, economic development policy group and included President Atwood and Frank Stanley, publisher of the *Louisville Defender*. As a result of years of often-heated discussions about Kentucky's future, the committee's final report recommended that the state desegregate its public schools.[78] The report did not by itself create immediate change, but it, too, forced upon whites a public consideration of imminent changes in Kentucky's racial segregation traditions.

As the committee published its recommendations, Hortense Young, a Louisville black activist and Republican politician, proposed to Louisville Mayor Charles Farnsley's Legislative Committee that it offer in the 1950 General Assembly a bill amending the Day Law. The bill as proposed would permit colleges in first-class cities, such as Louisville, to accept qualified students for graduate, professional, or vocational training regardless of race.[79]

In the 1950 legislative session, the black state representative from Louisville's Forty-Second House District, Jesse Lawrence, proposed a law similar to Young's proposal, one amending the Day Law to permit blacks to attend any institution if courses of equal quality were not available at Kentucky State.[80] Lawrence's bill passed, 50-16. Sponsored in the Senate by white Louisvillian Leon Shaikun, the amended Day Law passed without debate with a 23-to-3 tally. This dismantling of de jure segregation received quiet support from Governor Clements. The bill did not affect desegregation at other educational levels, and it left the responsibility for maintaining racial segregation to individual colleges. The legislature simply allowed each college to decide whether it wanted to desegregate, provided equivalent courses were not available at Kentucky State.

Significantly, the legislature avoided any definition of what constituted courses "equivalent" to those at Kentucky State.[81]

As a result, Kentucky private and public colleges loosely interpreted the ambiguous provisions of the new law to desegregate their campuses. Three Louisville Catholic colleges immediately opened their doors to blacks, publicly citing an absence of theology courses at Kentucky State as the reason. Berea College opened its doors under pressure from the Citizens Committee for the Repeal of the Day Law and the Berea Students for Democratic Actions, both anti–Day Law organizations.[82] Other Kentucky colleges, eager to be seen as progressive, announced policies permitting black student admissions. Nearly six hundred blacks later enrolled in Kentucky white colleges before 1954.[83]

Although the 1950 law was more successful than Young originally expected, some whites continued their efforts to circumvent desegregation. Residual support of segregation appeared in 1950 when the state became a member of the Southern Regional Compact, permitting Kentucky to share educational resources with other southern state governments. As mentioned earlier, the compact leaders proposed the purchase of Meharry Medical College. Acquisition by the compact member states of a regional, black medical school could prevent blacks from enrolling in white medical schools. As a countermeasure, publisher Frank Stanley of the *Louisville Defender,* Representative Jesse Lawrence, and Charles Steele, of the Louisville Urban League, lobbied for a state senate resolution that would forbid the compact's use as a segregation tool against Kentucky blacks. With the help of white Louisville legislators Leon Shaikun and Sidney Baer, the effort succeeded.[84]

With white legislative support and no opposition from Governor Clements, the modified Day Law escaped legal challenge. While "testing the waters" for desegregation, it also permitted blacks to matriculate at Kentucky white colleges that wanted to accept them. Along with this momentum for change, the U.S. Supreme Court issued on 5 June 1950 a ruling favorable to desegregation. In the cases of Heman Marion Sweatt and George W. McLaurin, it said that universities and colleges, regardless of racial designation, must provide the same treatment for students and that special all-black graduate programs established to avoid desegregation were unequal to those at white institutions.[85] As a sidebar to this controversy, activists, attorneys, and educators struggled to answer the question: Could an "inferior" black college ever be equal to a "superior" white college? Diverse academic programs and educator preferences complicated the efforts by local, federal, and supreme courts to decide whether black college programs were truly equal to their white counterparts. On their own, eight white Kentucky colleges had already determined that Kentucky State's curriculum was indeed different from but not inferior to their own and promptly admitted blacks under the amended Day Law.

With other private colleges admitting blacks, University of Louisville trustees decided on 19 April 1950 to implement their decision to desegregate. Under this policy change, the Louisville Municipal College closed in 1951, and its students enrolled at the University of Louisville or Kentucky State.[86] The closure of Louisville Municipal produced a personnel controversy, however, which continued until August 1951. At its center was the university's plan to merge the student population of Louisville Municipal with that of the main campus and fire the college's faculty with two months' severance pay. The plan drew criticism from the Louisville Municipal faculty and from the University of Louisville chapter of the American Association of University Professors. Although non-tenured faculty accepted the university's offer, tenured faculty objected. Sensing the university's hesitation to discuss their cases, the four tenured faculty employed local black attorney Harry McAlpin to represent their interests before the University of Louisville trustees.

After six months of private and public discussion of their upcoming separation from the University of Louisville, two of the tenured Louisville Municipal faculty members won a favorable resolution of their cases. Dr. Charles Parrish Jr. accepted an appointment as a University of Louisville "faculty advisor" to black students and was permitted to teach elective courses in sociology. Dr. Charles

Bright received a Ford Foundation Fellowship and one semester's pay of nine hundred dollars. Professors George D. Wilson and Henry S. Wilson refused the latter offer and continued to hold out for one month's pay for each year of service, or thirteen thousand dollars, each. Both men considered litigation as a solution.

Phillip Davidson, elected to the University of Louisville presidency in 1951, proposed to end the stalemate at the 18 May 1951 trustees' meeting by compromising with the black faculty holdouts. Reasoning that a long court battle might be detrimental to their personal interests and the process of desegregation, professors G.D. Wilson and H.S. Wilson agreed to accept Davidson's offer of forty-eight hundred dollars (one year's salary of University of Louisville professors of equal rank) plus nine hundred dollars each. The university also helped each to find employment elsewhere. George D. Wilson obtained a teaching position at Kentucky State through University of Louisville trustee Wilson Wyatt's personal contact with Gov. Lawrence Wetherby. Henry S. Wilson worked briefly at a black Louisville insurance company before accepting a teaching appointment in 1955 at a Louisville Catholic college.[87]

In these cases, university trustees used financial reasons to justify measured desegregation of University of Louisville, when a university study revealed that local sentiment would not oppose it. The majority of the trustees demonstrated an aversion to treating their black students and faculty equitably. That disposition influenced local black students, who often chose other in-state institutions for their undergraduate education.[88] As an alternative to the desegregated and possibly hostile institutions, Kentucky State persisted as the college that most specifically and amicably served the needs of the majority of the state's black students.

Kentucky State came under legislative scrutiny and periodic review, as did all public higher education. In order to discover the system's true condition, the General Assembly's Committee on Governmental Resources asked Dr. John D. Russell of the U.S. Federal Security Agency to conduct a nonpartisan study. The study team was charged to determine the prospects and needs of Kentucky public higher education without the political influence in college affairs so characteristic of twentieth-century Kentucky education.

Using an out-of-state team of five researchers, the study team reviewed each state college, including Kentucky State. In its report it recommended that Kentucky State drop "for Negroes" from its official name. It also recommended that Kentucky State have its own board of regents, thus placing it on the same statutory level as other state colleges. These recommendations, among others, received legislative approval in 1952.[89]

These actions suggested a willingness by state education officials and legislators to significantly improve the status of Kentucky State. Recognizing it as a peer of white public colleges and the University of Kentucky laid the foundation for Kentucky State's gradual acceptance as an equal institution of public higher education.

Although Kentucky State emerged as a public, independently governed, four-year college in 1952, the state continued to designate it informally as a state college reserved for blacks.[90] Despite that emphasis, the amended Day Law of 1950 allowed eight of Kentucky's forty historically white colleges and universities from 1950 to 1952 to enroll 456 blacks, including the 223 blacks merged into the University of Louisville from Louisville Municipal.[91]

In 1952 overt resistance to desegregation in Kentucky higher education remained strong at Paducah Junior College. This private school, established in 1932 by Paducah whites, refused to admit blacks on the grounds that the 1950 amended Day Law did not end racial segregation. College administrators declared that they risked prosecution if blacks were permitted to take courses equivalent to those at West Kentucky Vocational School. Buoyed by Lyman Johnson's victory over the University of Kentucky in March 1949, Paducah black students Fred A. Wilson Jr. and Henry Lee Powell, represented by Paducah NAACP attorney Joseph Freeland, sued the college in November 1949 as they sought admission.[92]

A 1938 state law that had removed all collegiate courses from West Kentucky Industrial and placed them at Kentucky State weakened Paducah Junior College's defense.[93] The successor to West

Kentucky Industrial College, West Kentucky Vocational School offered postsecondary vocational courses, none of which carried collegiate rank or resulted in certification. On 27 October 1950 federal district judge Roy A. Shelburne affirmed the right of qualified black students to attend Paducah Junior College on the grounds that the institution operated as a municipal college, that the failure to provide a separate but equal college for blacks deprived them of the equal protection of the law, and that the Day Law did not provide adequate defense for the college. Shelburne's decision effectively scuttled the Day Law as a defense in similar cases. He did not, however, find the act unconstitutional as the plaintiffs had hoped.[94]

After the order became public, plaintiffs Wilson and Powell received draft notices from the Paducah draft board.[95] Whether their sudden draft status was coincidental or planned by whites opposed to segregation is unclear. But Wilson and Powell's absence did not deter Curlee Brown, a black Paducah NAACP member. Brown and attorney Freeland found two other black Paducah college students, Marion Wilson and Eloise Broady Ray, who sought admission to Paducah Junior College in the fall 1951 term. The college refused their applications based on its interpretation of the amended 1950 Day Law. Here the college dean and board of trustees decided simply to ignore Judge Shelburne's order because it did not prescribe penalties for noncompliance. Subsequently, Paducah NAACP attorneys received permission from the federal district court, through *Fred A. Wilson, Jr. et. al. v. City of Paducah et. al.*, for Wilson and Ray to intervene.[96]

After hearing briefs from both sides, the U.S. District Court at Paducah issued a mandatory injunction perpetually enjoining Paducah Junior College from excluding qualified blacks. Recognizing defeat, the city of Paducah withdrew from the case. Nevertheless, in an attempt to continue resistance, Paducah Junior College won an indefinite stay of judgment on 25 January 1952 until the college appealed the decision to the Sixth Circuit U.S. Court of Appeals. After a year of waiting, the court of appeals upheld Shelburne's order. The college, faced with a costly and probably futile appeal to the U.S. Supreme Court, did not exercise its option to appeal. On 9 June 1953 four blacks registered without incident for the college's summer term.[97]

After two and one-half years of litigation, blacks had succeeded in gaining admission to Paducah Junior College and expanding the precedents against the Day Law's de jure segregation. Yet, the amended Day Law continued as a bulwark of segregated elementary and secondary schools. Opposition by blacks Jesse Lawrence, Frank Stanley, and Charles Steele and by whites Leon Shaikun, Sidney Baer, and others failed to nullify it. Although national NAACP attorneys warned Kentuckians to expect a decision favoring school desegregation from the U.S. Supreme Court in the 1954 spring term, the Kentucky General Assembly rejected a bill offered by Louisville white legislators Thelma Stovall and Charles McCann that would have simply repealed the 1950 amended Day Law.[98]

Continuing resistance to repeal implied that political and education leaders were unsure of Kentucky whites' acceptance of the prospect of public school desegregation. Governor Clements had not interfered with token desegregation in 1948 and 1950; the succeeding administration of Democratic governor Lawrence Wetherby had not taken any major steps toward school desegregation. The experimental nature of the amended Day Law and the fear of opposition from Kentucky whites constrained Wetherby to maintain the segregation policy consistent with his 1948 approval of the Southern Regional Compact's policies.

Wetherby's administration did obtain passage of the Minimum Foundation Program for Kentucky Public Schools, a measure that increased financial support for public elementary and secondary schools.[99] Superintendent of Public Instruction Wendell P. Butler later argued that such legislation proved fortunate because it helped public schools meet improvement and eventual desegregation costs.[100]

Given the continued white resistance, broad school desegregation did not come quickly to Kentucky. While Paducah Junior College reluctantly enrolled its first blacks in 1953, the U.S. Supreme Court studied the arguments and briefs of attorneys for Oliver Brown and twelve other black parents in Topeka, Kansas. They had filed suit to overturn a Kansas law that permitted racial segregation in public elementary and secondary schools. That case and three other school segregation cases from South Carolina, Virginia, and Delaware became known collectively as *Brown v. Board of Education.* On 17 May 1954 the Supreme Court ruled for the plaintiffs in those cases, declaring that "separate educational facilities are inherently unequal" and that the plaintiffs had therefore been denied due process of law.[101]

In a break with most southern governors, Governor Wetherby issued a brief statement confirming the state's compliance with the decision.[102] U.S. Senator Earle Clements, formerly governor of Kentucky, went one step further in his analysis. In an Omaha, Nebraska, interview, he called the decision "a fine thing," a directive that the state and the nation would obey. In addition, he believed that Democrats rather than the Republican administration of President Eisenhower should claim credit for it, since Democratic presidents had appointed eight of the nine Supreme Court justices and the action had begun during a Democratic administration.[103]

Clements's comments may have influenced Governor Wetherby. Although there is no clear causal relationship, within a week of Clements's statement, Wetherby established the Governor's Advisory Committee on Education Desegregation "to advise the state on problems ending segregation in public schools." Next, he appointed two blacks to the committee: Rev. Homer Nutter of Lexington and Earl Pruitt of Louisville.[104] Wetherby's biographer later argued that the governor's swift response reflected his true beliefs, previously hindered by the Day Law, and that his actions helped Kentucky to integrate its schools "with little acrimony." Wetherby's public support for desegregation ostensibly encouraged the Kentucky State Board of Education to urge public school districts to integrate their schools "as rapidly as conditions warrant." Wetherby's turnabout was also demonstrated in his refusal to sign a statement with other southern governors denouncing the ruling. Kentucky became one of five states with segregated schools (the others were Maryland, Tennessee, Arkansas, and West Virginia) whose governors refused to denounce desegregation.[105]

Following the lead that he and the State Board of Education offered, several Kentucky schools began slowly to desegregate. Early desegregation occurred in unexpected places. The public schools of sparsely populated Wayne County, Kentucky, for example, began desegregation in the summer of 1954.[106] In another surprise move, on 30 September 1954 Mrs. Geraldine Ogden, a Frankfort white, enrolled at Kentucky State after President Atwood announced that the college would admit white students. Ogden, who needed one course to complete her bachelor's degree at the University of Kentucky, withdrew one week later, citing a job opportunity in Lexington.[107] Later, Atwood urged other public institutions to reciprocate by admitting qualified black students.

Shortly thereafter, in the October/November 1954 issue of the *Kentucky Teachers Association Journal,* President Atwood extolled the virtues of an integrated Kentucky State. Two of his 1954 notions had remarkable accuracy as predictions of Kentucky State's future: it should direct its energies to serving the academic needs of state workers, and it should continue as a teacher education school. Both points became key parts of the institution's mission in the 1960s and 1970s.[108]

President Atwood's comments attempted to create a future direction for Kentucky State College, but he also recognized the whole system's need for improvement. At the time of his article, Kentucky ranked forty-seventh among the states in percentage of college-educated residents. Atwood also realized that desegregated colleges meant keener competition for black students. In 1954 only the best-prepared black students attended Kentucky's institutions, white or black. Whites enrolling at Kentucky State challenged it to become a more efficient college and academically competitive. On the other hand, the enrollment of white Kentucky State students strengthened Atwood's contention that it provided liberal arts curricula attractive to whites, but the school still needed to transcend the jim crow image fostered in the Day Law era. Kentucky State was therefore content to join a growing national trend among black colleges to aggressively recruit white students.[109] Briefly restated, desegregation meant the beginning of a new era requiring a nonracial raison d'être for Kentucky State. With the desegregation of historically white colleges and universities, Kentucky blacks had a wide choice of colleges. As able as he was to perceive the future, even Atwood could not predict the slow pace of desegregation that followed the *Brown* decision.

The 1954 *Brown* ruling initiated a new period in race relations in the United States. State laws requiring segregated education had become unconstitutional. Public school administrators were compelled to recognize that the "separate but equal" policy no longer had judicial support or legal mandate.[110] But the Supreme Court had not specified in what ways black schools and colleges should be made equal to white ones. Immediately before the Brown ruling, most southern states refused to engage in even minimal desegregation. From 1950 to 1954, court decisions had forced Missouri, Oklahoma, and Kentucky to desegregate their graduate and professional schools and undergraduate colleges. Token enrollments of black students on white campuses made the desegregation process more tolerable but not completely acceptable. Although Kentucky had tolerated minimal college desegregation since 1949, educators remained reluctant to desegregate until 1954. The University of Kentucky and the University of Louisville accepted black students in 1949 and 1950 respectively; other public colleges refused to follow their lead before the *Brown* decision.[111] A second *Brown* ruling in 1955 encouraged desegregation with "all deliberate speed," but still few blacks actually enrolled at Kentucky colleges.[112]

Kentucky's opposition to school desegregation appeared also at the grassroots level. Two early examples of this behavior occurred in 1955 in the western Kentucky towns of Clay and Sturgis. When black students wanted to enroll at all-white public schools, the resulting violent resistance by whites created national headlines. Both towns denied the blacks admission.[113] Faced with rebellion against both Supreme Court rulings, recently (November 1955) elected governor Albert B. Chandler sent National Guard troops and tanks to restore order and to permit black students to enroll without fear of violent attacks.

After the Clay and Sturgis incidents had demonstrated the state's disapproval of violent behavior, Kentuckians became more receptive to school desegregation. The Louisville public schools, under Superintendent Omer Carmichael, developed a plan for systemwide desegregation in the 1955-56 school year. Carried out in the fall of 1956 without conflict, the Louisville plan gave students freedom of choice; that approach served as a model for other southern urban school districts.[114]

These events coincided with another significant ruling affecting the desegregation of colleges and universities. In 1956 the Supreme Court issued a decision in *Florida ex rel. Hawkins v. Board of Control* that required colleges to give qualified black applicants "prompt admission."[115] Delay in desegregating colleges became unacceptable to the federal courts. No longer could segregationists find shelter in the ambiguous language of the *Fisher, Sweatt, McLaurin,* and *Brown* decisions. The Court stated clearly that colleges and universities *must* admit qualified black applicants.

Presented with these legal imperatives, Kentucky higher education faced the inevitable: complete public and private college desegregation. Under the Brown decision and the later litigation of 1956, the complete responsibility for segregation and desegregation shifted to college governing boards; it no longer fell on politically driven state legislators or governors.

The paucity of black enrollments at state colleges and universities clearly indicated continued acceptance of segregation. During the 1955-56 academic year, state regional colleges remained reluctant to admit blacks. However, presidents of the state's regional colleges wanted to desegregate their campuses. At a 23 November 1955 meeting of the Council on Public Higher Education, president Kelly Thompson of Western Kentucky State College moved that black students be admitted to all of the public colleges at once, effective during the 1956 summer term.[116]

One writer claimed that Morehead State College was "the first state college in Kentucky to admit Negroes" and the first to establish a policy to admit any person who met the admission requirements regardless of race. Such a statement ignored Kentucky State College and the few part-time black students at the University of Kentucky. Although the University of Kentucky blacks were enrolled in the smaller summer sessions when few whites were on the Lexington campus, the desegregation of the university preceded the desegregation of other white public institutions by seven years.[117]

The presence of the predominantly black Kentucky State encouraged the persistence of de facto segregation. Despite the assumption by white administrators that Kentucky blacks preferred the larger, predominantly white, colleges and universities, Kentucky State continued to draw many of the black students through the 1950s.[118]

Although the *Brown* decision was a moral and political victory for blacks, Kentucky State students were not immediately enthusiastic over the prospect of closely associating with persons who considered them inferior. Kentucky State attracted few white students after the *Brown* decision, and the black collegians remained loyal to the campus and traditions of Kentucky State.[119] Such perceptions fostered steady black enrollments at Kentucky State, which allowed Kentucky's predominantly white Kentucky colleges to remain so.

Later, as a new generation of black high school students, familiar with integrated settings, began to attend other Kentucky colleges, the need for a wholly black institution of higher education began to ebb. Pres. R.B. Atwood rightly perceived that black educational institutions and teachers would become casualties of desegregation. Still, he astutely recognized the persistence of southern white prejudices and black student preferences. Kentucky black leaders such as Atwood, Lyman Johnson, and Frank Stanley of the *Louisville Defender* preferred that racial discrimination and segregation end, but they did not push for immediate, widespread integration as the solution.

Instead, securing desegregation and establishing nondiscrimination in education, employment, housing, and public accommodations became their primary goals. To this extent Kentucky's black leaders continued their efforts to unravel the labyrinth of racially discriminatory state and local laws. The early token desegregation of Kentucky higher education permitted such Kentucky black leaders as James Crumlin and Hortense Young to attack other areas of persistent racial discrimination.

The movement of Kentucky higher education toward desegregation quickly generated a quiet, de facto segregation of black students at Kentucky State and did not encourage more blacks to enroll at Kentucky's white colleges and universities. Thereafter, Kentucky State administrators defined the college's mission as a desegregated, public liberal arts college concentrating on the education of both Kentucky blacks and local whites in state government in Frankfort.[120]

Epilogue: After 1954

THE POST-1954 ERA of Kentucky black higher education is characterized both by old traditions and by blacks' impatient demands for substantive change. Kentucky educators and politicians who formerly used higher education institutions to protect racial segregation strained to deconstruct the color line of 1904.

With the arrival of wider college-level desegregation and student-initiated sit-ins in 1960, Kentucky State no longer promoted itself as having an all-black student body. Before 1960 Kentucky State students and staff had avoided direct participation in the broader campaigns for civil rights, but as the nonviolent protest tactics of black student movements in Nashville and North Carolina became known, black Kentucky State students adopted them. Kentucky State administrators initially tolerated student sit-ins, protest marches, and demonstrations against Frankfort's businesses that practiced racial discrimination toward their black customers. A clash developed, however, when students observed President Atwood's moderate, conciliatory responses to local merchants who refused to desegregate their businesses. Frustrated by their lack of success with nonviolent protests, several hundred students rebelled in 1960 in a series of violent campus incidents. Although the white press and politicians supported Atwood in his suppression and ouster of the "student agitators," he opted to retire in 1962.[1]

Atwood's retirement marked the end of his remarkable contributions to black higher education. Described by his biographer as an "interracial diplomat," Atwood had benefited blacks and whites in different ways through his term as president. White governing boards from 1929 on perceived him as competent and apolitical in directing Kentucky's only public jim crow four-year college. Black leaders Charles Anderson and Albert E. Meyzeek, on the other hand, often opposed his collaborative activities with the segregationists that kept Kentucky State functioning. Alumni and student publications until the 1960s supported president Atwood as the key figure who championed the college's existence and who deflected local criticism of black higher education.[2]

The pace of change brought on by *Brown* and associated rulings did not mean that segregated higher education in Kentucky had suddenly disappeared. The controversy over Kentucky State's existence as the remaining legacy of segregated higher education continued for nearly two decades after Atwood's retirement. The parallel campaign of Kentucky blacks to achieve equal treatment at other institutions widened. Kentucky black students wanted white colleges to increase the presence of black faculty, staff, and curricula. University of Louisville black student sit-ins in the late 1960s produced confrontations with police. After the arrests of the students were resolved, the university responded by establishing a pan-African studies department and hiring more black faculty and staff.[3]

Other Kentucky black students then sought similar changes. Pres. Otis Singletary at the University of Kentucky appointed Robert Zumwinkle as vice president for student affairs in 1970, and one of his first assignments was to resolve black student issues. Using two faculty and staff volunteers, the university opened the Office of Minority Affairs in 1971.[4] The last state university created in the state, Northern Kentucky University, developed in 1987 an Afro-American studies program. Although black students accounted for less than 2 percent of the total student population, the university created the program following their expressions of concern about the poor quality of campus race relations. According to one observer, this program "made a significant impact on the institution, whether it is acknowledged or not by history writers." The controversy over the Afro-American studies program intimated that the institution was not free of institutional racism although it began as a state college in 1968, fourteen years after the *Brown* ruling.[5]

State officials charged with desegregating higher education directed their energies toward Kentucky State College and its successor, Kentucky State University. Since 1952 many college-bound Kentucky black students made it their first choice. As indicated in earlier chapters, other institutions, such as the University of Louisville, the University of Kentucky, Eastern Kentucky State College, Morehead State College, Murray State College, Western Kentucky State College, and the private colleges did not attract large numbers of black students in the early years of desegregation.

When Dr. Carl M. Hill was inaugurated as president of Kentucky State in 1962, supporters hoped he would transform the college in the same way that President Atwood did in 1929. Hill, a chemistry professor and former dean of arts and sciences at Tennessee State University, worked to enroll more local white students and state workers as suggested by President Atwood in 1954. Yet, Frankfort newspaper critics portrayed the campus as a "negro" college campus that should be merged into the University of Kentucky community college system. This not-too-subtle effort to close Kentucky State produced protracted opposition by alumni, faculty, staff, and friends.[6]

After several months of extended discussion in the Frankfort press on this issue, the legislature responded by approving increased appropriations for the college. The intent was to improve both the facilities and curricula and expand both black and white student enrollments. Although more whites enrolled in Kentucky State's evening division, the campus retained a predominantly black full-time student body with an emphasis on liberal arts programs.

In 1968 Kentucky State black students reacted angrily to the assassination of Dr. Martin Luther King by attacking sporadically several businesses adjacent to the campus. After these incidents newspaper editorials urged the legislature and the Council on Higher Education to reconsider the merger of Kentucky State into the University of Kentucky. Again, alumni and Kentucky's black community leaders responded by channeling their political support and pressure for Kentucky State to remain a freestanding, four-year college.[7]

A massive self-study in 1969 for accreditation by the Southern Association of Colleges and Schools suggested that new programs were again needed to define clearly Kentucky State's mission and role in the Kentucky system of higher education. Supported by the self-study visitation committee recommendations, the regents and the administration obtained legislative relief through enactment of a statute permitting the college to become a university on 1 July 1972. Under this law Kentucky State University offered its own graduate courses in public affairs for state workers seeking to improve their skills and could award its own graduate degrees—a very different picture from that of the 1940s, when it could offer graduate courses but not award degrees. President Atwood's 1952 predictions about Kentucky State's future mission finally came to fruition.

The physical and academic development of Kentucky State University continued at a measured pace while other Kentucky higher education institutions gradually attracted more Kentucky blacks. The increasing black presence at the University of Kentucky and the University of Louisville could be attributed to the creation of offices for minority affairs at both institutions. Although hampered by limited funding, both operations pushed their respective institutions to add black studies curricula and to recruit more black faculty, staff, and students. The four regional state universities hired token black faculty to complement the growing numbers of black students. By 1980 the Commonwealth assumed that the vestiges of the Day Law's 1904 color line had been largely destroyed via court rulings, a 1966 state civil rights act, and their actions in the late 1960s and 1970s. The federal courts and the federal government did not agree.

An effort to correct these misconceptions developed from out-of-state events in the late 1970s. Beginning in 1977, a series of lawsuits broadly called the *Adams* cases required southern and border states to dismantle former dual systems of higher education based on race.[8] The court rulings required the U.S. Department of Education's Office of Civil Rights to review those states that had maintained dual systems of higher education. In January 1981 the U.S. Department of Education announced that Kentucky State University and the other

five state universities continued to practice subtle de facto racial segregation in student recruitment and in the hiring of black faculty and
staff. Thereafter, the state of Kentucky was required to develop a plan
to end de facto segregation in higher education or risk losing all federal support.[9]

As in the student upheavals in the 1960s and 1970s, a simplistic
solution reappeared: close the mostly black Kentucky State and shift
its resources (and students) to the mostly white public institutions.
For the third time, alumni, student, staff, and community groups organized a campaign to save Kentucky State.[10]

Interestingly, senior civil rights activist Lyman Johnson did not
agree. His support for Kentucky State University's closure hinged on
the belief that the institution, if continued, would evolve into a predominantly white college and the dollars allocated to Kentucky State
would be better spent aiding students at other public universities. His
opposition notwithstanding, Kentucky's black leaders galvanized
support in the public hearings on this issue for the retention of
Kentucky State University as a freestanding, historically black but integrated, institution.[11]

In its written response to the U.S. Department of Education, the
state proposed that it would meet numerous goals and objectives for
desegregation. Among them was the recruitment of more blacks to
predominantly white institutions and more whites to Kentucky State.
Since 1975 the gradual transformation of Kentucky State into a predominantly white university often encountered obstacles.[12]

Dr. William A. Butts, the successor to Carl M. Hill, who retired
as Kentucky State University's president in 1975, took a more pro-
active stance in defending the institution as a historically black but
integrated institution. A highly respected political scientist and sea-
soned university administrator, Butts engaged in an intensive effort to
win more appropriations for the university from the state legislature
in competition with other state university presidents.[13]

Butts's reforms of the institutional and physical structures were
sidetracked by incidents of violent black student behavior, rising out-
of-state student enrollments, and increasing costs. Compounding

these problems were shortfalls in the state revenue that meant brutal budget reductions for all universities, including Kentucky State. With the public support for his efforts to meet these challenges dwindling and two votes of no confidence by the faculty, he resigned the presidency effective 1 July 1982.[14]

His replacement was Raymond M. Burse, a black member of the Council on Higher Education and a proponent of the plan to retain Kentucky State University as a freestanding institution while meeting the desegregation criteria of the U.S. Department of Education. A practicing attorney in Louisville, a Rhodes scholar, a graduate of both Centre College of Kentucky and the Harvard University Law School, Burse had never held an administrative or faculty position in a higher education institution. Under the desegregation plan, he quickly obtained several million dollars to transform the institution's physical appearance and introduce new elements to its academic and physical organization. New faculty and staff were hired to operate the university's innovative Whitney M. Young College of Liberal Studies, which attracted outstanding black and white students from its designated service area of central Kentucky.

Burse's plan to maintain Kentucky State as the "small, liberal arts state university" enjoyed initial external financial support and attracted new benefactors. The prospect of a revised institutional mission and policies, however, led to internal disputes among faculty and staff about President Burse. These events, including several dismissals of key administrative staff, became public as many of the faculty and staff grew dissatisfied with his aggressive and—as described in the press—contentious "management style."[15]

On 24 March 1989 Burse announced his resignation. He pointed out that under his leadership the university had created the Whitney Young College of Liberal Studies, which attracted outstanding students; improved institutional fund-raising; increased student retention; and established campus-wide data and word processing capabilities. Dr. Mary Levi Smith, academic vice president of Kentucky State, was appointed by the regents as interim president until a search committee found a permanent successor.[16]

On 9 March 1990 the regents announced that Dr. John T. Wolfe, provost and vice president at Bowie State University in Maryland, was to become the tenth president of Kentucky State University effective 1 July 1990. Like his immediate predecessors, he wanted to make his mark on the campus and the commonwealth. He sought new academic programs and facilities and widened recruitment efforts for white and black students.[17] Professionally trained and respected internationally as a linguist, he adapted to the Kentucky culture quickly and won friends for himself and the university until September 1991.

The press reported at that time that President Wolfe had deleted the names of five key administrators from the list of administrators to be recommended for annual contracts by the regents. Board of regents chair and former governor Louie B. Nunn, who wanted certain Kentucky State University administrators not rehired, sought to clarify these personnel matters with the president. Subsequently, the board discovered that Wolfe had made repairs to the president's residence without complete board approval and had submitted a pay increase for himself to the regents. In an uncanny repeat of the scenario surrounding the forced resignation of Green P. Russell in 1929, the regents took depositions from Wolfe and twenty other officials at an off-campus attorney's office. On 28 September 1991 the *Louisville Courier Journal* reported that the regents had asked Wolfe to cancel plans for his delayed formal inauguration and resign. Wolfe refused.[18] Students, alumni, and friends expressed concern about these events. On 6 October 1991 Rev. Jesse Jackson of the National Rainbow Coalition, who had visited Kentucky State in the 1980s, returned and asked for a massive prayer vigil before the regents met to decide President Wolfe's fate. The vigil did not materialize.

On 7 October 1991 the regents formally charged President Wolfe with incompetence, immoral conduct, and neglect of duty. These charges were based on his self-proposed pay raise (any salary increase for the president is the prerogative of the regents) and his bidding of improvements to the president's residence in amounts less than ten thousand dollars and thus avoiding board approval. Student and alumni concern over the charges led to calls by them to Gov. Wallace Wilkinson for the dismissal of the board of regents and its chair. He refused. On 12 October 1991 a brief sit-in at the administration building by a small group of students during the homecoming weekend heightened tensions. As a hearing (required by statute) on the charges began on 18 October 1991, Wolfe announced that he had resigned both the presidency and his tenured professorship.

The settlement allowed Wolfe to serve as a consultant to Kentucky State's executive vice president, Mary L. Smith, and released both the board and Wolfe from current or future liability. Wolfe shortly moved to Washington to work for Reverend Jackson's National Rainbow Coalition.[19]

Again, academic vice president Mary L. Smith served as interim president. Without engaging in an external search, the board voted six to three on 30 October 1991 to approve Dr. Smith as Kentucky State's eleventh president. With her acceptance, she became only the second female and the first black woman to head a public college in Kentucky.[20]

The saga of post-1954 Kentucky black higher education was one of constant struggle to obtain equal and not extraordinary treatment. While the predominantly white colleges and state universities received encouragement for their desegregation efforts, Kentucky State continued to be the center of the "race problem" in higher education and the subject of never-ending scrutiny, suspicion, and concern by the press and oversight agencies. The small numbers of black students on the white campuses remained largely quiescent, with the exception of black athletes, whose presence helped the University of Kentucky in 1978 and 1996 and the University of Louisville in 1980 and 1986 to win national basketball championships.

Access by Kentucky blacks to higher education became a nagging "race problem" begging for a quick and painless solution. As the white politicians and their black critics had admitted since 1900, the twentieth-century color line had become a social enigma of immense proportions. Black and white leaders often found it difficult to reach a reasonable middle ground, given a half-century of legal segregation and several additional decades of "deliberate speed" in achieving complete desegregation. It became apparent that the racial barrier fed on collective societal delay. More precisely, this procrastination postponed the achievement of improved educational opportunity for blacks and hindered the efforts to remove racism's blot from the American social fabric. The Commonwealth of Kentucky, as one of the oldest seams of that fabric, held on doggedly to the concept that civil or "genteel" racism was preferable to the civil rights for all guaranteed by the U.S. Constitution. When the state finally turned away from enforcing racial discrimination as public policy, it reacted slowly to the courageous efforts of certain blacks and whites who were committed to complete equality of educational opportunity under law. Their individual untold stories are the missing pieces in the continuing puzzle of Kentucky race relations.

Appendix

Table 1. Black and White Population in Kentucky, 1870-1950

Year	Percent of blacks to whites in total population	Whites	Blacks
1870	16.8	1,098,692	222,210
1880	16.5	1,377,179	271,451
1890	14.4	1,590,462	268,071
1900	13.4	1,862,309	284,706
1910	11.4	2,027,951	261,656
1920	9.8	2,180,462	226,040
1930	8.6	2,388,364	235,938
1940	7.5	2,631,425	214,031
1950	6.9	2,726,022	201,921

SOURCES: 1870-1910: U.S. Bureau of the Census, *Negro Population* (Washington, D.C.: Government Printing Office, 1918). 1920-30: U.S. Bureau of the Census, *Negroes in the United States, 1920-1932* (Washington, D.C: Government Printing Office, 1932). 1940: U.S. Bureau of the Census, *Sixteenth Census of the U.S., 1940: Population Volume: Characteristics of the Population* (Washington, D.C.: Government Printing Office, 1943). 1950: U.S. Bureau of the Census, *Census of the Population: 1950,* vol. 2, *Characteristics of the Population,* pt. 17, "Kentucky" (Washington, D.C.: Government Printing Office, 1952).

Table 2. 1917-1918 State Appropriations for Black and
White Colleges and Normal Schools in Selected Southern
and Border States

State	Black percent of total	Black	White
Alabama	18	20,000	91,000
Arkansas	11	2,000	99,426
Georgia	0	0	237,500
Kentucky	12	21,000	150,000
Louisiana	0	0	68,750
Maryland	13	10,000	70,000
Mississippi	0	0	54,500
Missouri	7	33,682	464,966
North Carolina	7	22,449	278,200
Oklahoma	12	50,537	378,957
South Carolina	34	64,500	122,490
Tennessee	33	26,659	53,319
Texas	16	142,297	772,881
Virginia	13	32,250	210,133
West Virginia	21	51,850	189,425

SOURCE: U.S. Department of the Interior, Bureau of Education, *Biennial Survey of Education,* bulletin 1919, vol. 4, no. 91, 1916-18 (Washington, D.C.: U.S. Government Printing Office, 1921), 89-93, 100-105.

NOTE: Delaware, District of Columbia, and Florida were not reported in the set of data. This table excluded state-supported universities. States were not consistent in identifying colleges or normal schools. Hence, aggregate appropriations are provided.

Table 3. 1927 State Appropriations for Black and White
Teachers Colleges and Normal Schools in Selected
Southern and Border States

State	Black percent of total	Black	White
Alabama	19	74,475	322,708
Arkansas	34	76,506	147,853
Georgia	7	25,071	347,388
Kentucky	4	70,000	1,711,795
Louisiana	24	140,000	433,017
Maryland	6	44,020	695,854
Mississippi	12	40,677	292,829
Missouri	10.2	127,661	1,243,371
North Carolina	26	207,346	586,248
Oklahoma	11	182,500	1,501,000
South Carolina	52	122,336	112,836
Tennessee	14	165,000	1,003,000
Texas	11	271,169	2,281,905
Virginia	28	240,278	622,011
West Virginia	1.5	11,000	716,500

SOURCE: U.S. Department of the Interior, Office of Education, *Biennial Survey of Education, 1926-1928,* bulletin 1930, no. 16 (Washington, D.C.: U.S. Government Printing Office, 1930), 898, 928-31, 944-45.
NOTE: Delaware, District of Columbia, and Florida were not reported. Data excludes state universities. States were not consistent in identifying colleges or normal schools. Hence, aggregated data is indicated.

Table 4. 1937-1938 State Appropriations for Black and White Colleges in Selected Southern and Border States

State	Black percent of total	Black	White
Alabama	30.4	150,575	344,336
Arkansas	19.9	46,433	185,761
Delaware	17	60,667	296,571
Georgia	13	267,188	1,784,385
Kentucky	3	66,500	2,305,391
Louisiana	4	278,889	6,059,020
Maryland	24	418,630	1,328,744
Mississippi	3	55,233	1,883,453
Missouri	7	356,143	5,032,818
North Carolina	27	1,096,186	2,933,024
Oklahoma	4	293,728	7,055,607
South Carolina	13	240,442	1,564,921
Tennessee	8	110,171	1,264,921
Texas	2	150,947	8,982,714
Virginia	9	256,680	2,705,793
West Virginia	16	326,500	1,671,688

SOURCE: U.S. Office of Education, Federal Security Agency, *Biennial Survey of Education in the United States, Statistics of Higher Education, 1937-38,* bulletin 1940, no. 2, chap. 4 (Washington, D.C.: U.S. Government Printing Office, 1942), 194-237.

Table 5. Illiteracy in Kentucky for Persons Ten Years Old
and Older among Blacks and Whites, 1900-1930

Group	1900	1910	1920	1930
Total population	2,147,174	2,289,905	2,416,630	2,614,589
White illiterates	174,768	150,097	112,206	102,962
Black illiterates	88,137	57,900	40,548	28,553
Percentage of white illiterates in total population	8.1	6.5	4.6	3.9
Percentage of black illiterates in total population	4.1	2.5	1.6	1.0

SOURCES: U.S. Bureau of the Census, *Thirteenth Census of the United States, 1910: Population* (Washington, D.C.: U.S. Government Printing Office, 1913), 2:725; *Fourteenth Census of the United States, 1920: Population* (Washington, D.C.: U.S. Government Printing Office, 1923), 3:666; U.S. Bureau of the Census, *Negroes in the United States 1920-1932* (Washington, D.C.: U.S. Government Printing Office, 1932), 734.

Table 6. Highest Grade Completed by Kentucky Blacks and Whites Twenty-Five Years Old and Older, 1940 and 1950

Group	1940		1950	
	Total	Percent of total	Total	Percent of total
Population (all ages)	2,845,627	100.00	2,944,806	100.00
Blacks	214,031	7.52	201,921	6.85
Whites	2,631,425	92.47	2,742,090	93.11
Population (25 years and older)				
Blacks	118,405		124,259	
Whites	1,434,100		1,316,675	
College (1-3 years)				
Blacks	2,573	2.1	3,430	2.9
Whites	57,519	4.4	79,065	5.5
College (4 years)				
Blacks	2,039	1.6	2,630	2.2
Whites	40,444	3.1	56,380	3.9

SOURCES: U.S. Bureau of the Census, *Sixteenth Decennial Census, 1940: Population Characteristics* (Washington, D.C.: Government Printing Office, 1943), 2:5, 191; *Seventeenth Decennial Census, 1950* (Washington, D.C.: Government Printing Office, 1952), 2:17-32.
NOTE: The question on illiteracy addressed in previous censuses was deleted and replaced by a question on the highest grade completed.

Table 7. Initial Admission of Blacks to Publicly Supported Kentucky Colleges and Universities, 1904-1954

Name and years of operation	Location	Year of first black admission
Kentucky State University[*]	Frankfort	1886
Louisville Municipal College for Negroes (1931-51)	Louisville	1931
University of Kentucky (1865 to present)	Lexington	1949
University of Louisville (1798 to present)	Louisville	1950
West Kentucky Industrial College for Colored Persons (1909-38)	Paducah	1909

[*] Also known as Kentucky State Normal School for Colored Persons (1886-1902), Kentucky Normal and Industrial Institute for Colored Persons (1902-26), Kentucky State Industrial College for Colored Persons (1926-38), Kentucky State College for Negroes (1938-52), and Kentucky State College (1952-72). The name Kentucky State University has been used since 1972.

Table 8. Initial Admission of Blacks to Privately Supported Kentucky Colleges and Universities, 1904-1954

Name and Years of Operation	Location	Year of first black admission
Berea College	Berea	1855-1904, 1950
Bellarmine College	Louisville	1950
Eckstein Norton Institute	Cane Springs	1890-1911
Lincoln Institute*	Lincoln Ridge	1910
Louisville Presbyterian Theological Seminary	Louisville	1950
Nazareth College	Louisville	1950
Simmons University**	Louisville	1879
Southern Baptist Theological Seminary	Louisville	1950
Ursuline College	Louisville	1950

* The junior college division closed in 1932.

**Also known as Kentucky Theological and Normal Institute (1879-81) and State Colored Baptist University (1881-1918).

Notes

Introduction

1. James D. Anderson, *The Education of the Blacks in the South, 1860-1935* (Chapel Hill: Univ. of North Carolina Press, 1988), 4-32. Armstrong and Washington's influence on industrial education is discussed in Henry A. Bullock, *A History of Negro Education in the South* (New York: Praeger, 1970), and Louis R. Harlan, *Booker T. Washington: The Making of a Black Leader, 1856-1901* (New York, Oxford University Press, 1972). Washington's autobiographical work, *Up from Slavery* (New York: Doubleday, 1902), reveals his personal vision of industrial education as the ultimate "solution" for African American economic and social survival.

2. Constitution of Kentucky, sec. 187.

3. J. Morgan Kousser, "Making Separate Equal: Integration of Black and White School Funds in Kentucky," *Journal of Interdisciplinary History* 10, no. 3 (winter 1980): 399-428. This process occurred in some Kentucky communities the following year. See Lee A. Dew, *"Claybrook v. Owensboro:* An Early Victory for Equal Educational Opportunity in Kentucky," *Daviess County Historical Quarterly* 8, no. 1 (Jan. 1990): 2-15.

4. Henry C. Weeden, *Weeden's History of the Colored People of Louisville* (Louisville: Published by the author, 1897), 34.

5. Anderson, *Education of Blacks,* 13; Marion B. Lucas, "Kentucky Blacks: The Transition from Slavery to Freedom," *Register of the Kentucky Historical Society* 91, no. 4 (autumn 1993): 408, 415-16.

6. L.H. Williams, *Black Higher Education in Kentucky,* 51-53.

7. Marrs, *Life and History,* 119-25; William H. Ballew, Diamond Jubilee (Louisville: American Baptist, 1943), 104.

8. Acts of the General Assembly, 1883-84, chap. 650, pp. 1182-84.

9. *Circular of Information for the Twenty-First Annual Session Eckstein Norton Institute, Incorporated* (Cane Spring, Ky.: Institute Press, 1911), 26-27, Simmons Bible College Records, University of Louisville Archives.

10. Acts of the General Assembly, 1885-86, chap. 1297, pp. 232-35; J.A. Hardin, *Onward and Upward,* 3.

11. Superintendent of Public Instruction, Commonwealth of Kentucky, Common Schools Reports, 1893, 71, Kentucky Department of Libraries and Archives.

12. G.C. Wright, *History of Blacks in Kentucky,* 103-51.

13. Acts of the General Assembly, 1893, chap. 211, p. 963, chap. 239, p. 1209; 1896, resolution no. 6, p. 76; 1897, chap. 21, p. 33.

14. G.C. Wright, *History of Blacks in Kentucky,* 110. For a brief sketch of Louisville's black high school see Thelma Cayne-Tilford-Weathers, *A History of Louisville Central High School, 1882-1982* (Louisville: Published by the author, 1982), 1-3. See also S.E. Smith, ed., *History of the Anti–Separate Coach Movement of Kentucky* (Evansville, Ind.: National Afro-American Journal and Directory Publishing Co., 1894[?]).

1. Hardening the Color Line

1. The Berea College experience continues to be the subject of scholarly examination. See James M. McPherson, *The Abolitionist Legacy* (Princeton, N.J.: Princeton Univ. Press, 1975), 244-61; Peck, *Berea's First Century,* 1-38.

2. Paul David Nelson, "Experiment in Interracial Education at Berea College, 1858-1908," *Journal of Negro History* 59 (Jan. 1974): 13-27.

3. Andrew E. Murray, *Presbyterians and the Negro: A History* (Philadelphia: Presbyterian Historical Society, 1966), 200-201; McPherson, *Abolitionist Legacy,* 253.

4. The story of Day's perception of Berea College students and their racial egalitarianism came from William E. Barton, vice president of the college board of trustees. See *Boston Transcript,* 18 June 1904. The Kentucky constitution was amended in 1866 by section 187, which required that white and black children be educated separately in the public schools.

5. The legislative history of the Day bill can be found in the *Journal of the House,* 18 Feb. 1904, 526-27; *Journal of the Senate,* 11 March 1904, 1052-53; Acts of the General Assembly, 1904, chap. 85, p. 181.

6. Peck, *Berea's First Century,* 54. Berea catalogs from 1905 to 1909 described the rationale and effort to provide separate but equal education for blacks: "The Kentucky Legislature has passed a bill prohibiting private schools from receiving both white and colored students and from attending any school where both races are received. The Trustees of Berea College have been advised that this law is in contravention of the provision of the Federal constitution, and violated the civil rights not only of the Negro but of every citizen of the United States. The College will endeavor to have the law declared unconstitutional, and appeal to the Supreme Court of the United States

if necessary. . . . Under existing conditions, however, no colored students can be received at Berea. Those formerly enrolled will be assisted to attend Fisk University and good schools." See William G. Frost, *For the Mountains* (New York: F.H. Revel Co., 1937), 177.

7. *Berea College v. Commonwealth of Kentucky,* 94 S.W. 623-29. The decision contained the dates of the original indictment and its statutory basis. The one-thousand-dollar fine levied on the college would eventually be returned to the college. See *Berea Citizen,* 4 Feb. 1909.

8. *Berea College v. Commonwealth of Kentucky,* 94 S.W. (1906) 629.

9. Ibid., 628.

10. Ibid., 629.

11. Ibid.; *Berea College v. Commonwealth of Kentucky,* 211 U.S. (1908), 58.

12. *Berea College v. Commonwealth of Kentucky,* 211 U.S. (1908), 58. The decision's language supports segregation by supporting the power of a state to regulate private corporations and avoids the race question implicit in the Day Law: "The Court of Appeals, while striking it down, sustained the balance of the act. We need concern ourselves only with the inquiry, whether the first section can be upheld as coming within the power of a State over its own corporate creatures. . . . We are of the opinion, for reasons stated, that it does come within that power, and on this ground the judgement of the court of Appeals of Kentucky is affirmed" (58).

13. Ibid., 69. Harlan's dissent on the ruling has become a classic statement against the logic of segregation laws: "Have we become so inoculated with prejudice of race that an American government, professedly based on principles of freedom, and charged with the protection of all citizens alike, can make distinctions between such citizens in the matter of their voluntary meeting for innocent purposes simply because of their respective races? Further, if the lower court be right, then a state may make it a crime for white and colored persons to frequent the same market places, at the same time, or appear in an assemblage of citizens convened to consider questions of a public or political nature in which all citizens, without regard to race, are equally interested" (69).

14. *Berea Citizen,* 11 Feb. 1904; *Boston Transcript,* 18 June 1904, 19 Jan. 1905; *New York Evening Post,* 25 Feb. 1907; *Indianapolis Freeman,* 5 Dec. 1908.

15. *Berea Citizen,* 11 Feb. 1904.

16. See McPherson's treatment of Berea College in his *Abolitionist Legacy;* Nelson, "Experiments in Interracial Education at Berea College," 13-27; Burnside, "Suspicion versus Faith." All of these works discuss Frost's antiblack and prowhite sympathies at Berea.

17. Printed letter "To those interested in the Negro's rights in Berea

College, Sept. 5, 1904," from A.W. Titus and Josie C. Woodford, W.M. Young Papers.

18. *Indianapolis Freeman,* 5, 26 Dec. 1908.

19. Ibid., 4 July 1908.

20. U.S. Department of the Interior, *Reports of the Commissioner of Education* (Washington, D.C.: Government Printing Office, 1890-1909).

21. *Reports of Commissioner of Education,* 1909, 1027.

22. The "new Berea" (Lincoln Institute) story can be found in several places: *Lincoln Institute Worker,* 1 March 1909, 1, in the Berea College Archives; *Berea Citizen,* 9 April 1908; G.C. Wright, "Founding of Lincoln Institute"; Barksdale Hamlett, *History of Education in Kentucky* (Frankfort, Ky.: State Journal Co., 1914), 326-27; *Indianapolis Freeman,* 29 May 1909.

23. *Indianapolis Freeman,* 30 Jan. 1909.

24. Ibid., 30 Jan. 1909, 16 Dec. 1911.

25. Ibid., 7 March 1908.

26. Ibid., 5 Dec. 1908.

27. *Berea College v. Commonwealth of Kentucky,* 123 Ky. 209, 623-29; *Lexington Leader,* 29 June 1911.

28. Lowell H. Harrison, ed., *Kentucky's Governors, 1792-1985* (Lexington: Univ. Press of Kentucky, 1985), 90.

29. *Indianapolis Freeman,* 24 April 1909.

30. Ibid., 18 Sept. 1909.

2. Acceptance of Civil Racism

1. James S. Hathaway to Booker T. Washington, 19 Jan., 29 Oct. 1901, reel 269, Washington Papers. This reel also contains several letters from John H. Jackson to Washington following Jackson's resignation from the Kentucky State presidency in 1898.

2. *Indianapolis Freeman,* 26 Dec. 1908.

3. Ibid., 29 May 1909; Acts of the General Assembly, 1910, chap. 10, pp. 38-40; *Columbia Trust Co. v. Lincoln Institute of Kentucky,* 129 S.W. 113-17.

4. *Indianapolis Freeman,* 26 Dec. 1908.

5. Ibid., 30 Jan. 1909.

6. Ibid., 9 Jan. 1909.

7. *Proceedings of the Kentucky Negro Education Association,* 1915, Louisville, 1915, 63, Kentucky State Univ. Blazer Library Archives (hereafter cited as KSU-BLA).

8. Ibid., 62.

9. Charles Henry Parrish, ed., *Golden Jubilee of the General*

Association of Colored Baptists in Kentucky (Louisville: Mayes Printing Co., 1915), 182-84; Negro History Bulletin 5 (Jan. 1942): 91-93.

10. For data on Eckstein-Norton Institute, see *Circular of Information,* 26-27.

11. William Decker Johnson, *Biographical Sketches of Prominent Negro Men and Women of Kentucky* (Lexington: Standard Print, 1897), 22-23; Parrish, Golden Jubilee, 284-85.

12. *Indianapolis Freeman,* 22 June 1907.

13. Ibid., 8 March 1908.

14. J.A. Hardin, *Onward and Upward,* 5.

15. Raymond Randles, "A Biography of the Norton Family" (master's thesis, Univ. of Louisville, 1961); *Louisville Courier-Journal* 13 Jan. 1893.

16. Acts of the General Assembly, 1902, chap. 33, p. 71; "Biennial Report of the Superintendent of Public Instruction, July 1899 to June 30, 1901," in "Biennial Report of the Superintendents of Public Instruction," Superintendent of Public Instruction Files, Kentucky Department for Libraries and Archives, Frankfort, Ky. (hereafter cited as SPI-KDLA).

Kentucky State also enlarged its buildings and physical plant by the construction of a dormitory for female students and the purchase of a farm, which permitted male students to practice their agricultural skills. The campus, located near the Frankfort city limits, gradually received improvements from the General Assembly. For an extended discussion of the State Normal School and Kentucky Normal and Industrial periods, see J.A. Hardin, *Onward and Upward,* 1-15.

17. "State Normal School for Colored Persons," in *Kentucky Public Documents—Common School Reports,* 1903 (Frankfort: Commonwealth of Kentucky, 1903), 86.

18. "Biennial Report of Pres. John H. Jackson, Kentucky Normal and Industrial Institute for Colored Persons," in *Kentucky Public Documents—Common School Reports,* 1907 (Frankfort: Commonwealth of Kentucky, 1907), 328.

19. *Indianapolis Freeman,* 27 June 1908.

20. William T. Turner, "History of Hopkinsville (M & F) College: Nearly a Century of Religious Training, 1883-1973," Austin Peay State Univ., 1973, unpublished photocopy of typescript from the author; Thomas Jesse Jones, ed., *Negro Education: A Study of the Private and Higher Schools for Colored People in the United States,* vol. 2 (Washington, D.C.: Government Printing Office, 1917), 277.

21. *Paducah Sun-Democrat,* 15 Sept. 1929.

22. Acts of the General Assembly, 1918, chap. 18, pp. 55-58; *Journal of the Senate,* 1918, 129; pamphlet by E.E. Reed, "Reasons for the

Establishment of a Western State Normal and Industrial Institute for Negroes: A Letter to the Members of the General Assembly of Kentucky" (Bowling Green: Kentucky State Negro Educational Association, Jan. 1, 1916).

23. *Pittsburgh Courier,* 17 May 1924.

24. Kentucky Educational Commission, *Public Education in Kentucky* (New York: General Education Board, 1921), 187; Kentucky Efficiency Commission, *The Government of Kentucky* (Frankfort: Commonwealth of Kentucky, 1924), 408; *Louisville Courier-Journal,* 26 April 1931; Oscar R. Galloway, "Higher Education for Negroes in Kentucky" *Bulletin of the Bureau for School Service of the University of Kentucky* 5, no.1 (Sept. 1932): 131-32.

25. "West Kentucky College for Colored Persons Board of Trustees Minutes, 1924-1934," 58, 80, 83, in SPI-KDLA.

26. *Louisville Leader,* 13 Dec. 1919; George Dewey Wilson, "A Century of Negro Education in Louisville," Louisville Municipal College Files, Univ. of Louisville Archives, 1941, typescript, 144-46.

27. *Louisville Leader,* 15 Jan. 1921; G.D. Wilson, "A Century of Negro Education," 144; "Report of the Board of Trustees of Simmons University," 16 Aug. 1919, in Simmons Bible College Records, Univ. of Louisville Archives (hereafter cited as SBCR).

28. *Louisville Courier-Journal,* 11 June 1925.

29. Ibid., 31 Oct., 15 Dec. 1922.

30. Series 4, Nov. 1922, SBCR.

31. Fenton, *Politics,* 48-49; George Brown Tindall, *The Emergence of the New South, 1913-1945* (Baton Rouge: Louisiana State Univ. Press, 1967), 219-53.

32. Lamon, *Black Tennesseans,* 59-109.

33. Acts of the General Assembly, 1883-84, vol. 1, chap. 650, pp. 1182-84.

34. *Louisville Post,* 30 Oct. 1923.

35. Miscellaneous Records, series 4, n.d., SBCR.

36. *Louisville News,* 17 April 1926.

37. Ibid., 15 May 1924.

38. *Louisville Herald,* 30 May 1925; *Louisville Courier-Journal,* 19 June 1925.

39. *Louisville Post,* 13 July 1925.

40. *Indianapolis Freeman,* 19 Feb. 1910.

41. *Louisville Herald,* 6 Dec. 1925; "The Record of Albert Ernest Meyzeek," *Negro History Bulletin* 10 (May 1947): 186-97; G.C. Wright, *Life behind a Veil,* 163, 167-68.

42. T.J. Jones, *Negro Education,* 41-42. Meyzeek, a Toledo, Ohio,

native of white Canadian and black American parents, received his under-graduate training at Indiana State Normal College and his graduate education at Indiana University at Bloomington. In 1893 Meyzeek assumed the princi-palship of both Louisville Central Colored High School and Louisville Colored Normal School. *Louisville Leader,* 6 Sept. 1924; *Indianapolis Freeman,* 20 Aug., 3 Sept. 1910. Consult Meyzeek's biography by Horton, *Old War Horse,* 7-19.

43. *Indianapolis Freeman,* 3 Sept. 1910.

44. Ibid., 20 Jan. 1912.

45. Ibid., 10 Feb. 1912.

46. Ibid., 17 Feb., 16 March 1912.

47. Ibid., 13, 20 July, 3 Aug. 1912.

48. Ibid., 6 July 1912.

49. Ibid., 17 Aug. 1912.

50. Ibid.; *Lexington Weekly News,* 17 Aug. 1912.

51. *Indianapolis Freeman,* 5 Oct. 1912.

52. Ibid.

53. *Louisville Courier-Journal,* 20 Oct. 1914; "Education," Crisis 9 (Dec. 1914): 62.

54. Timberlake, *Politics and the Schools.*

55. Russell's 1913 and 1917 reports to the superintendent of public in-struction defend the application of industrial education at Kentucky State. See Superintendent's Reports for 1913 and 1917, SPI-KDLA.

56. *Hopkinsville New Era,* 12 March 1921; *Louisville Leader,* 9 April 1921.

57. *Lexington Herald,* 6 May 1923.

58. Ibid. See also Kentucky Normal and Industrial Institute for Colored Persons, "Minutes," 17 March 1923, KDLA, 193.

59. *Lexington Herald,* 6 May 1923.

60. John E. Wood also served as the national president of the National Baptist Convention in 1923 and 1924. See *Indianapolis Freeman,* 2 Sept. 1924.

61. *Lexington Herald,* 20 May 1923.

62. Ibid. See also Thomas D. Clark, *History of Kentucky* (Lexington: Bradford Press, 1977), 444.

63. "Memorandum [on] Reorganization of the Kentucky Normal and Industrial Institute," in *Annual Catalogue of the Kentucky Normal and Industrial Institute 1921-1924* (Frankfort, Ky.: 1923), 11-21. For data on Wood, see W.D. Johnson, Biographical Sketches, 10; Dunnigan, Black Kentuckians, 180; *Louisville Leader,* 22 May 1943.

64. G.D. Wilson, "A Century of Negro Education," 157.

65. William E. Ellis, "Catholicism and the Southern Ethos: The Role Of Patrick Henry Callahan," *Catholic Historical Review* 69, no. 1 (Jan. 1983): 41-50; G.D. Wilson, "A Century of Negro Education," 150; George C. Wright, "Black Political Insurgency in Louisville: The Lincoln Independent Party of 1921," *Journal of Negro History* 68 (winter 1983): 14.

66. *Louisville Leader,* 12 Nov. 1921; G.C. Wright, "Black Political Insurgency," 17.

67. G.D. Wilson, "A Century of Negro Education," 2, 8, 15, 47; G.C. Wright, "Black Political Insurgency," 19; Federal Writer's Project, *A Centennial History of the University of Louisville* (Louisville: Univ. of Louisville, 1939), 187. According to his biographer, Albert E. Meyzeek was the individual "who placed before [the University of Louisville trustees] an outline of what was wanted [by the ad hoc committee]." See Horton, *Old War Horse,* 15.

68. Federal Writer's Project, *Centennial History,* 212; G.D. Wilson, "A Century of Negro Education," 158-59.

69. Acts of the General Assembly, 1926, chap. 90, pp. 304-5.

70. "Kentucky Normal and Industrial Institute for Colored Persons, Minutes of Board of Trustees Financial Records and Letters, 1914-1929," 16 July 1928, 351; 30 July 1928, 360; 31 Oct. 1928, 374-75; 20 Nov. 1928, 435-36. Burch's allegations are found in two reports: "Report A—Nov. 13, 1928" and "Report B—Nov. 1928." Russell's responses to Burch's comments are found in "Adjustments Suggested in Accountant's Report," 10 Dec. 1928. These documents are in SPI-KDLA.

71. "Minutes of the Board of Trustees of KSIC, 1929-1934," 1, SPI-KDLA.

72. *Commonwealth of Kentucky v. Green P. Russell,* 19 Sept. 1929, cases 4499, 4500, 4501, box 2548, Franklin County Circuit Court Docket, Kentucky Department for Libraries and Archives, Frankfort, Ky. (KDLA).

73. *Louisville Courier-Journal,* 12 April 1930; *Louisville News,* 19 April 1930; L.M. Coleman, "Kentucky State College," 27-28.

74. *Waukegon (Illinois) News-Sun,* 19 Oct. 1936; *Chicago Defender,* 31 Oct. 1936. For a detailed description of the Green P. Russell and Francis Marion Wood eras, see J.A. Hardin, "Study in Politics and Race."

75. D.O.W. Holmes, *The Negro College,* 187-89. For an updated analysis of this issue see Anderson, *Education of Blacks.*

76. Dwight O.W. Holmes, *The Negro College,* 185; William T.B. Williams, *Report on Negro Universities in the South* (Trustees of the John F. Slater Fund, 1913), 2-3; U.S. Department of the Interior, Bureau of Education, *Survey of Negro Colleges and Universities,* bulletin 1928, no. 7 (Washington, D.C.: Government Printing Office, 1929), 1-5; Horace Mann Bond, *The*

Evolution of the Negro in the American Social Order (New York: Prentice-Hall, 1934), 364-65.

3. Hopes, Reforms, and Resistance

1. Federal Writer's Project, *Centennial History,* 212.
2. "University of Louisville Board of Trustees minutes," 13 Jan., 9 June 1930, Univ. of Louisville Archives.
3. Louisville Municipal College Bulletins, 1931-42, Louisville Municipal College Files, Univ. of Louisville Archives.
4. Atwood argued that Kentucky State had been a traditional site for political patronage jobs for blacks. See Rufus Ballard Atwood, "Segregation to Integration: The Administration of the Presidency of Rufus Ballard Atwood at Kentucky State College at Frankfort, KY from 1929 to 1962," 1964, chap. 1, Atwood Papers.
5. H.S. Smith, "Kentucky State College" Wilberforce University Quarterly Kentucky Normal and Industrial College minutes, 1929; Atwood, "Segregation to Integration." For an expanded study of Atwood's efforts, see G.L. Smith, *A Black Educator.*
6. Atwood, "Segregation to Integration," chap. 3, p. 16.
7. Ibid.
8. U.S. Department of the Interior, Office of Education, *Effects of the Depression upon Public Elementary and Secondary Schools and upon Colleges and Universities,* bulletin 1937, no. 2 (Washington, D.C.: Government Printing Office, 1938), 54; Acts of the General Assembly, 1934, chap. 65.
9. U.S. Department of the Interior, Office of Education, *Statistics of Higher Education,* 1931-1932, bulletin 1933, no. 2 (Washington, D.C.: Government Printing Office: 1935), 126, 159; U.S. Department of the Interior, Office of Education, *Statistics of Higher Education,* bulletin 1935, no. 2 (Washington, D.C.: Government Printing Office, 1937), 122, 162.
10. Ibid. Both sources.
11. Ibid.
12. *Kentucky Thorobred,* 10 Nov. 1930, KSU-BLA.
13. Ibid., vol. 7, no. 7 (May 1932): 1.
14. Ibid., vol. 3, no. 1 (Sept.-Oct. 1932): 1-3; vol. 3, no. 3 (Dec. 1932): 1-3; vol. 3, no. 5 (Feb. 1933): 1.
15. *Ten Year Report of Kentucky State College,* 1929-1939 (Frankfort: Kentucky State College, 1939), 29, KDLA. For an overview of the cultural life on Kentucky State's campus, see J.A. Hardin, *Onward and Upward,* 88-90.

16. *Ten Year Report,* 22-47.

17. Ibid., 63.

18. Federal Writer's Project, *Centennial History,* 214; H.W. Peters, "Report of the Superintendent of Public Instruction," *Commonwealth of Kentucky Educational Bulletin* 7, no. 9 (Nov. 1939): 40-43.

19. *Kentucky Educational Bulletin* 1, no. 7 (Sept. 1933): 144; D.O.W. Holmes, *The Negro College,* 198-99.

20. Federal Writer's Project, *Centennial History,* 213.

21. Ibid., 214; *Louisville Courier-Journal,* 17 July 1937.

22. Kentucky Efficiency Commission, *Government of Kentucky,* 408.

23. Ibid.

24. Murrell, "Paducah Junior College," 36; *Paducah Sun-Democrat,* 1 Nov. 1936.

25. *Kentucky Negro Education Journal* 9, no. 1 (Jan.-Feb. 1938): 21-22; R.B. Atwood to A.B. Chandler, 5 Nov. 1937, box 72, Chandler Papers.

26. G.D. Wilson's comments are found in his typescript autobiography, "Footprints in the Sand," University of Louisville Archives.

27. "Minutes of the Kentucky State Board of Education," book 6, 15 Aug. 1935, 74, SPI-KDLA.

28. *New York Times,* 4 Dec. 1936.

29. *Louisville Courier-Journal,* 18 March 1937; *Louisville Leader,* 4 Dec. 1937.

30. *Pittsburgh Courier,* 12, 19 July 1934; A.E. Meyzeek and Lee L. Brown to T. Arnold Hill, 30 July 1934, C. Eubank Tucker to Hill, 8 Aug. 1934, Hill to Meyzeek, 10 Aug. 1934, ser. 4, box 31, National Urban League Papers, Manuscript Division, Library of Congress. See also *Louisville Leader,* 17 Nov. 1935.

31. Charles W. Anderson to Walter W. White, 20 Jan. 1936, NAACP Papers.

32. Acts of the General Assembly, 1936, chap. 43, pp. 110-12.

33. *Chicago Defender,* 10, 31 July, 28 Aug. 1937; *Pittsburgh Courier,* 6 Nov. 1937.

34. Acts of the General Assembly, 1934, chap. 65.

35. *Louisville Courier-Journal,* 13 Dec. 1937.

36. Ibid., 15 Dec. 1937, 6 Jan. 1938. See also "Minutes of the State Board of Education of the Commonwealth of Kentucky," 17 Dec. 1937, KDLA.

37. *KNEA Journal* 9, no. 1 (Jan.-Feb. 1938): 21-22; R.B. Atwood to A.B. Chandler, 5 Nov. 1937, box 72, Chandler Papers. The internal controversy and attendant problems are discussed later in this chapter.

38. *Louisville Leader,* 19 March 1938.

39. Acts of the General Assembly, 1938, chap. 29, pp. 1083-91.

40. Kentucky Educational Commission, *Public Education in Kentucky;* Kentucky Efficiency Commission, *Government in Kentucky.*

41. A.B. Chandler, interview.

42. For comment on the quality of southern higher education, see Tindall, *Emergence of the New South,* 497-99. A contemporary study labeled only seven institutions in the south "adequately staffcd and equipped" for the doctorate. See American Council for Education, *Report on Committee on Graduate Instruction* (Washington, D.C.: American Council for Education, 1934), 4-35.

43. McVey, *The Gates Open Slowly,* 209-11. For a critical essay on Kentucky's persistent reluctance to finance education, see Thomas D. Clark, "Kentucky Education through Two Centuries of Political and Social Change," *Register of the Kentucky Historical Society* 83, no. 3 (summer 1985): 173-201.

44. U.S. Department of the Interior, Office of Education, *Education of Negroes: A Five Year Bibliography, 1931-1935,* bulletin 1937, no. 8 (Washington, D.C.: Government Printing Office), 20.

45. W.E.B. Du Bois, "The Negro College,' *Crisis* 40 (Aug. 1935): 175; Robert R. Moton, "Negro Higher and Professional Education in 1943," *Journal of Negro Education* 2 (July 1933): 397-402; Thompson, "Negro Higher Education," 257-71.

46. John A. Pollard, "Consolidating the Colleges," *School and Society* 34 (19 Sept. 1931): 404-8; Charles H. Thompson, "Are There Too Many Negro Colleges?" *Journal of Negro Education* 3 (April 1934): 159-66.

47. For an extended examination of this issue, see C.S. Johnson, *Negro College Graduate.*

48. *Ten Year Report,* 61-63.

49. Ibid., 64-65.

50. L.T. Johnson, interview, 22 May 1984.

51. Perry, interview, in Black Louisville Oral History Project, Univ. of Louisville Archives.

52. *KNEA Journal* 9, no. 1 (Oct.-Nov. 1938): 32.

53. Ibid.

54. *KNEA Journal* 9, no. 1 (Jan.-Feb. 1938): 19-20.

55. Ibid., 17-20.

56. *Missouri ex. rel. Gaines v. Canada,* 305 U.S. 337, 345 (1938). The NAACP attorneys argued that states were required to provide equal education according to the "separate but equal" precedents. Segregation per se was not challenged. The university's counsel argued that segregation was not at issue.

57. *Louisville Courier-Journal,* 31 Dec. 1938; *KNEA Journal* 9, no. 2 (Jan.-Feb. 1939): 7.

58. Albert B. Chandler to Frank McVey, Paul Garrett, James

Richmond, Raymond Kent, Harry Peters, Frank Peterson, R.E. Jaggers, D.A. Lane, A.E. Meyzeek, J.A. Thomas, C.W. Anderson, R.B. Atwood, W.H. Fouse, S.L. Barker, H.L. Donovan, W.H. Humphrey, 29 June 1939, box 72, Chandler Papers.

59. *Louisville Courier-Journal,* 12 March 1939.

60. "Minutes of the Governor's Advisory Committee on Equalizing Educational Opportunity," 24 Nov. 1939, group 1, box C-200, NAACP Papers.

61. "State Education Committee Recognizes Right of Negroes to Attend Kentucky U.," 1 Dec. 1939, news release, NAACP Papers.

62. "Minutes of the Governor's Advisory Committee," 1; Mark Ethridge to Walter White, 14 Dec. 1939, NAACP Papers. Following the issuance of the committee's final report on 7 March 1940, the legislature and the governor all but ignored the committee's recommendations for partial desegregation of the state's white colleges.

63. "Minutes of the State Board of Education," 15 March 1940, 9:93, KDLA. See also Lewis N. Taylor, "Negro Education in Kentucky," *Commonwealth of Kentucky Department of Education Bulletin* 11, no. 3 (May 1943): 177.

64. Thurgood Marshall to Charles Anderson, 5 April 1939, Charles Anderson to Charles H. Houston, 8 Feb. 1939, group 1-C-200, NAACP Papers; *Louisville Leader,* 4 Feb. 1939.

65. R.B. Atwood to Walter White, 14 March 1939, NAACP Papers.

66. Acts of the General Assembly, 1936, chap. 43, pp. 110-12. The law was never revised but allowed the legislature to renew the stipends awarded to blacks for their out-of-state graduate education.

67. "Report of the Superintendent," 42. Among these schools were Harvard, Columbia, Chicago, Ohio State, Michigan, Wisconsin, Minnesota, New York University, Cornell, Iowa State, and Cincinnati. The largest enrollments in the summer of 1939 were at Fisk University (29), Indiana University (23), University of Cincinnati (12), and the University of Michigan (11). The remaining thirty schools had 8 or fewer students each.

68. "Minutes of the Governor's Advisory Committee," 2.

69. For a comparison of Kentucky expenditures with those of other southern states in three randomly selected years, please consult tables 2, 3, and 4 in the Appendix.

4. Separate and Unequal

1. McVey, *The Gates Open Slowly,* 250; J.W. Brooker, "Biennial Report of the Superintendent of Public Instruction," (Frankfort: State Board of Education, 1941).

2. For a definition of illiteracy, see U.S. Bureau of the Census, *Thirteenth Census of the United States, 1910: Population* (Washington, D.C.: Government Printing Office, 1913), 2:721, 725. See also *Fourteenth Census of the United States, 1920: Population* (Washington, D.C.: Government Printing Office, 1923), 3:366, 434. *Negro Population 1790-1915* (Washington, D.C.: Government Printing Office, 1918), 428; *Negroes in the United States, 1920-1932* (Washington, D.C.: Government Printing Office, 1932), 293, 734; *Abstract of the Fifteenth Census of the United States* (Washington, D.C.: Government Printing Office, 1933), 279-81. For outmigration and birth rate data, see A. Lee Coleman, Albert C. Pryor, and John Christiansen, *The Negro Population at Mid-Century,* bulletin 643, June 1956, Univ. of Kentucky Agricultural Experiment Station, Lexington, 24-27.

3. Clark's comment refers to the Constitution of Kentucky, 1891, secs. 91, 9.3.

4. Thomas D. Clark, "Kentucky Education," 195-96; Mary Helen Miller, ed. *A Citizen's Guide to the Kentucky Constitution,* Legislative Research Commission Report 137, July 1981, Frankfort, Ky., 113-14.

5. U.S. Bureau of the Census, *Sixteenth Decennial Census, 1940: Population Characteristics* (Washington, D.C.: Government Printing Office, 1943), 2:5, 191, pts. 1-7, table 13. For data on years of school completed by persons twenty-five years old and over in 1940 and 1950 see U.S. Bureau of the Census, *Seventeenth Decennial Census,* 1950 (Washington, D.C.: Government Printing Office, 1952), 17-23, table 20.

6. Gordon F. DeJong and George A. Hillery Jr., *Kentucky's Negro Population in 1960,* bulletin 704, Nov. 1965, Univ. of Kentucky Agricultural Experiment Station, Lexington, 6.

7. NAACP press release, 8 November 1940, NAACP Papers.

8. Yolanda Barnett to Thurgood Marshall, 24 Sept. 1940, NAACP Papers.

9. *Valla Dudley Abbington et. al. v. Louisville Board of Education,* Civ. 243, W.D. Ky. (1941).

10. *Louisville Courier-Journal,* 7, 8, 9 Dec. 1940.

11. Prentice Thomas to Thurgood Marshall, 14 Dec. 1940, NAACP Papers.

12. John A. Miller to Joseph D. Scholtz, 21 Dec. 1940, NAACP Papers.

13. *Louisville Courier-Journal,* 27 May 1941; Louisville Kentucky Teachers' Salary Case, April 1941, Miscellaneous Legal Files, NAACP Papers; William T. Baskett to Prentice Thomas, 30 Sept. 1941, NAACP Papers; Amended Answer of Plaintiffs in *Abbington v. Board of Education,* 3 Oct. 1941, Legal Files, NAACP Papers. For another perspective on this issue, see G.C. Wright, *History of Blacks in Kentucky,* 162-68. For an extended

discussion of similar cases, see Bruce Beezer, "Black Teachers' Salaries and the Federal Courts before *Brown v. Board of Education:* One Beginning for Equity," *Journal of Negro Education* 35, no. 2 (1986): 200-213.

14. Prentice Thomas to Thurgood Marshall, 14 Feb. 1941, NAACP Papers.

15. Ibid.; Prentice Thomas to Charles Houston, 23 June 1941, NAACP Papers.

16. Prentice Thomas to Thurgood Marshall, 18 June 1941, NAACP Papers.

17. Prentice Thomas to Thurgood Marshall, 31 July 1941, NAACP Papers.

18. *Louisville Courier-Journal,* 14 Sept. 1941; *Charles Lamont Eubanks v. Herman Lee Donovan,* Petition for Writ of Mandamus, Fayette Circuit Court, 13 Sept. 1941. Eubanks's attorneys withdrew this petition and instituted a new suit for damages and an injunction. See *Eubanks v. Donovan,* Civ. 215, E.D. Ky. (1941). His attorneys hoped the federal courts would be more willing to accept change.

19. "Minutes of the State Board of Education," 5 Nov. 1941, 145-46, KDLA. This section recorded board approval for a civil engineering program that "Governor Keen Johnson and President H.L. Donovan of the University of Kentucky, Lexington, were extremely anxious for the State Board to give . . . consideration." The resolution supporting this program was presented by J.W. Brooker, superintendent of public instruction and board chairman. The resolution said, "Application has been made for work in civil engineering and no work available in this field at the present time." The resolution also stated that the requirements of the "curriculum be comparable in every respect to that offered for the same two years at the University of Kentucky." The board quickly and unanimously approved the measure.

20. Charles H. Houston, "Eubanks Case Notes," 20 Nov. 1943, group 2, B-199, NAACP Papers. His notes described his visit on 18 Nov. 1943 with the Kentucky State "school of engineering" faculty and the University of Kentucky engineering dean.

21. The extensive correspondence between the attorneys defending the University of Kentucky is found in group 2, B-199, NAACP Papers. Most of the correspondence concerns the attorneys' meeting procedural demands of the U.S. marshal and the assistant attorney general of Kentucky, amending the original complaint, requesting postponements because of unforeseen personal problems, and Eubanks's and his attorneys' inability to appear in court when necessary.

Eubanks's attorneys also changed during prosecution of the case. Thurgood Marshall, Charles H. Houston, Prentice Thomas, and John Rowe also served on the case. Serving of summonses, pleadings, and presentation of attorney credentials added to the confusion regarding the case. For a specific chronology of events see group 2, B-199, NAACP Papers.

22. Prentice Thomas to Mrs. Bodie Henderson (Eubanks's mother), 17 March 1943; Prentice Thomas to S.A. Burnley, 24 March 1943, group 2, B-199, NAACP Papers.

23. Charles Eubanks to Prentice Thomas, 20 July 1943; Charles H. Houston, summary of Eubanks case to 20 Nov. 1943, group 2, B-199, NAACP Papers. Houston's summary indicated that the change in attorneys general caused by the election of a new governor should not affect the case. However, the defendants attacked Eubanks's suit on new grounds, especially since Kentucky State and the University of Kentucky offered civil engineering courses.

24. See Houston's summary for a description of Kentucky State's program. He perceived the instructor in the program as having a "poor" academic record. See 11 Nov. 1943, group II, B-199, NAACP Papers.

25. *Journal of the Senate,* 1944, H.B. 245, p. 988.

26. Ibid., vol. 2, H.B. 265, p. 1203.

27. Ibid.

28. Ibid., p. 1907.

29. *Louisville News,* 11 March 1944.

30. Charles W. Anderson to Milton R. Konvitz, 2 March 1944; telegram, Charles W. Anderson to Thurgood Marshall, 7 March 1944, Miscellaneous Legal Files, NAACP Papers; Charles Anderson to Roy Wilkins and Thurgood Marshall, 18 March 1944, NAACP Papers.

31. *Louisville News,* 11 March 1944.

32. Lyman T. Johnson to Roy Wilkins, 2 March 1944, Miscellaneous Legal Files, NAACP Papers.

33. Press release attached to letter from Charles Anderson to Roy Wilkins and Thurgood Marshall, 16 March 1944, NAACP Papers.

34. Forty-one members of the House supported the Anderson bill, and forty opposed it. See *Journal of the House of Representatives,* 1944, 1909-11.

35. The *Journal of the Senate,* 1944, mentioned the bill as being referred to the rules committee for study. It was not discussed again.

36. *Eubanks v. Donovan,* Civ. 215 E.D. Ky. (1941), 8 Jan. 1945; *Louisville Defender,* 13 Jan. 1945.

37. Thurgood Marshall to Charles Houston, 16 Jan. 1945, group 2, B-199, NAACP Papers.

38. Affidavit, filed 20 Jan. 1945, U.S. District Court, Eastern District of Kentucky; Charles H. Houston to Charles W. Anderson, group 2, B-199, NAACP Papers.

39. The NAACP branch files of the NAACP Papers reveal that the Henderson, Lexington, Paducah, and Louisville branches had begun to de-

velop a statewide organization, in contrast with their method of operation during their first two decades. See Louis P. McHenry to Thurgood Marshall, 20 Feb. 1950, Kentucky Branch Files, NAACP Papers. For a personal recollection of the Lexington branch activities, consult William S. Dotson, recorded interview, 23 Jan. 1983, Blacks in Lexington Project, Special Collections, Univ. of Kentucky Library.

40. *Louisville Defender,* 13 Nov. 1945. For Atwood's comments on the press role creating the "fights" between black leaders, see his "Segregation to Integration," chap. 4, p. 30, Atwood Papers.

41. *Smith v. Allwright,* 321 U.S. 69 (1944).

42. Gunnar Myrdal, *An American Dilemma* (New York: Harper and Brothers, 1944), 1021-24.

43. Rudolph, *American College and University,* 483-96. For a more critical evaluation of modern American higher education since World War II, see Jencks and Riesman, *Academic Revolution.*

44. President Truman's Executive Order no. 9981, 3 C.F.R. 722 (1948), and its subsequent effects have been treated by Charles C. Moskos Jr. in "Racial Integration in the Armed Forces," *American Journal of Sociology* 72 (Sept. 1966): 132-48.

45. Louisiana Acts, 1946, no. 142, p. 412; *Wilson v. Board of Supervisors,* 92 F. Supp. 986-88 E.D. Louisiana (1950); U.S. Commission on Civil Rights, *Equal Protection of the Laws in Public Higher Education 1960* (Washington, D.C.: Government Printing Office, 1960), 22-23.

46. *Wrighten v. Board of Trustees,* 72 F. Supp. 948 E.D. S.C. (1947); South Carolina Acts, 1945, no. 223, p. 401, 1947, p. 622; *New York Times,* 22 Nov. 1947; U.S. Commission on Civil Rights, *Equal Protection,* 23.

47. See also "Meeting of the Commission on Negro Affairs, October 7, 1945, Frankfort, Kentucky," in series 5, box 55, National Urban League Papers.

48. *The Report of the Kentucky Commission on Negro Affairs,* November 1, 1945 (Frankfort, Ky., 1945), 30.

49. Ibid., 9-11. This section addressed the complex educational problems of Kentucky blacks.

50. *Commission on Negro Affairs,* 30.

51. Ibid.

52. Ibid., 31. Several weeks after the report became public, Dean William Funkhouser of the University of Kentucky Graduate School admitted that "Kentucky must adopt a definite policy in keeping with the law and inherent democratic rights.... Kentucky must choose between a dual system of professional and graduate schools or admit Negro students to existing courses." See *Louisville Leader,* 1 Dec. 1945.

53. An editorial in the 18 Nov. 1945 *Louisville Courier-Journal* criti-

cized the expenditure of $157,000 for black higher education in Kentucky while white colleges received nearly $4 million for four state colleges and one state university.

54. *Louisville Courier-Journal,* 18 Nov. 1945

55. Ibid.

56. Ibid., 1 Dec. 1945.

57. *New York Times,* 10 Aug. 1946, 15; *Pittsburgh Courier,* 4, 11 Aug. 1945. In another incident, two former Kentucky State students in Frankfort were arrested for assaulting an off-duty state policeman. When a mob of five hundred whites gathered outside the police headquarters, some remarked that "these niggers have beaten-up a highway patrolman and we ought to hang them." Judge L. Boone Hamilton ordered the blacks sent to a Lexington jail and set bond at twenty thousand dollars. Within three days, the two were returned, found guilty by Hamilton of misdemeanor assault, and fined fifty-five dollars plus court costs. This event was the second "racial flare-up" in Frankfort in 1946. See *Louisville Courier-Journal,* 24 April 1946; *Lexington Herald-Leader,* 24 April 1946; *Frankfort State Journal,* 24 April 1946, 29, 30 Oct. 1946.

58. L.T. Johnson, interview, 21 May 1984.

59. L.T. Johnson, interview, Black Louisville Oral History Project, Univ. of Louisville, 5 May 1976; *Pittsburgh Courier,* 7 Feb. 1948.

60. *Louisville Leader,* 13 April 1946. Anderson's attempt for reform was labeled as the "Little Civil Rights Bill." See *Chicago Defender,* 14 Feb. 1948.

61. *Louisville Leader,* 13 Dec. 1947.

62. Clarence L. Timberlake maintained a cordial relationship with Clements as late as 1972. Timberlake also served on the Kentucky Negro State Coordinating Committee, which was organized to lend support to desegregation efforts after the *Gaines* decision. See Timberlake to R.B. Atwood, 4 Dec. 1941; Timberlake to Earle Clements, 24 March 1951, 26 Jan. 1972; Earle Clements to Timberlake, 4 Feb. 1972, Clarence L. Timberlake Papers, Special Collections, Murray State Univ.

5. Desegregated but Still Separate

1. Horton, *Not without Struggle,* 21, 23.

2. U.S. Bureau of the Census, *Sixteenth Census of the United States, 1940: Population Characteristics* (Washington, D.C.: Government Printing Office, 1943), 2:305, 318-19.

3. *Pittsburgh Courier,* 7 Feb. 1948; *Louisville Leader,* 7 Feb. 1948.

4. *Louisville Defender,* editorial, Oct. 1950, in Clarence L. Timberlake Papers.

5. *Sipuel v. Board of Regents,* 332 U.S. 631 (1948). See also *Sipuel v. Board of Regents,* 180 P. 2d. 135 Okla. (1947).

6. Jean L. Preer, *Lawyers v. Educators, Black Colleges and Desegregation in Public Higher Education* (Westport, Conn.: Greenwood Press, 1982), 79; Fisher v. Hurst, 333 U.S., 150.

7. Preer, *Lawyers v. Educators,* 79-81.

8. Ibid.

9. *Pittsburgh Courier,* 14 Feb. 1948.

10. Ibid.

11. Ibid., 13, 20 March, 15 May 1948; *Chicago Defender,* 24 April, 1 May 1948; *Louisville Leader,* 30 March 1948. Walter White attempted to persuade black organizations to testify on the issue in March 1948. Not all black leaders were interested. See telegram to Lester Granger, executive secretary, National Urban League, from Walter White, 9 March 1948; memorandum from Lester Granger to Lloyd Garrison, 14 March 1948, series 1, box 35, National Urban League Papers.

12. *Chicago Defender,* 22 May 1948.

13. *Pittsburgh Courier,* 7 Feb. 1948; *Louisville Leader,* 17 Jan. 1948; L.T. Johnson, interview, 22 May 1984.

14. Lyman T. Johnson served as president of the Louisville Branch of the NAACP. In separate interviews, Johnson argued that the branch made such a commitment. See also Roy Wilkins to Lyman T. Johnson, 29 Feb. 1944, group 2, B-199, NAACP Papers. Wilkins encouraged the branch to continue in the fight because "it was an organization which carried the *Gaines* case against the University of Missouri to the United States Supreme Court. We have been in the middle of this fight to open up state universities to Negro students and certainly our leading branch in Kentucky ought to be in the forefront of this particular fight." Wilkins to Johnson, 29 Feb. 1944.

15. Maurice F. Seay to Lyman T. Johnson, 24 March 1948, group 2, B-90, NAACP Papers; *Louisville Times,* 24 March 1948.

16. *Pittsburgh Courier,* 3 April 1948.

17. Minutes of the State Board of Education, 13 July 1948, book 18, 203-8. The board approved the idea, with its black member, Albert E. Meyzeek, voting no on the entire procedure. The board was notified by telegram on 9 July 1948 "that an emergency situation to make provision for more adequate higher educational advantages for Negroes demanded their attention. Minutes of the State Board of Education, 13 July 1948, 203.

18. Thomas Hamilton Syvertsen, "Earle Chester Clements and the Democratic Party, 1920-1950," (Ph.D. diss., Univ. of Kentucky, 1982), 345-47. For another view of this incident, see Talbert, *University of Kentucky,* 174-76.

19. U.S. Commission on Civil Rights, *The Black/White Colleges,* 5; Rufus Clement, "Legal Provisions for Graduate and Professional Education of Negroes in States Operating a Separate School System," *Journal of Negro Education* 8 (1939): 144-47. For another view, see U.S. Commission on Civil Rights, *Equal Protection,* 21-23.

20. *Louisville Courier-Journal,* 12 Sept. 1948.

21. *Louisville Leader,* 17 July 1948; *Baltimore Afro-American,* 24 July 1948.

22. *Louisville Leader,* 4 Sept. 1948.

23. L.T. Johnson, interview, 22 May 1984.

24. For a discussion of the inadequacy of state funding of Kentucky higher education, see Howard W. Beers, *Kentucky: Designs for Her Future* (Lexington: Univ. of Kentucky Press, 1945), 246-49. Beers contended that Kentucky contributed less toward higher education than its neighboring states. If the state wanted to make economic progress, it needed to support higher education and in particular, the University of Kentucky, in a more favorable light.

25. *Louisville Leader,* 12 June 1948; *Baltimore Afro-American,* 26 June 1948.

26. *Sweatt v. Painter,* 339 U.S. 629, 635-36 (1950).

27. Lyman T. Johnson to Walter White, 5 Jan. 1949, NAACP Papers.

28. Ibid.; Lyman T. Johnson to Thurgood Marshall and Louis P. McHenry, 15 Jan. 1949; Memorandum from Marion Wynn Perry to Robert L. Carter and Franklin L. Williams, 17 January 1949, NAACP Papers.

29. Robert L. Carter, memorandum to files, 23 Feb. 1949, NAACP Papers.

30. Ibid.

31. L.T. Johnson, interview, 22 May 1984.

32. Ibid.

33. W.L. Kean, president of Louisville Association of Teachers in Colored Schools, to members, 1 March 1949, NAACP Papers.

34. L.T. Johnson, interview, 22 May 1984.

35. Robert Carter to Ben Shobe, 5 April 1949, NAACP Papers.

36. *Baltimore Afro-American,* 18 Sept. 1948; *Louisville Courier-Journal,* 12 Sept. 1948.

37. *New York Times,* 21 Oct. 1948.

38. Thomas D. Clark, 14 June 1978, from alumni/faculty, Oral History Project, Department of Special Collections and Archives, Univ. of Kentucky Libraries.

39. *Louisville Courier-Journal,* 25 Sept., 15 Nov. 1948.

40. President Atwood formally presented his objections to the State

Board of Education on 17 Dec. 1948. See Minutes of the State Board of Education, book 19, 17 Dec. 1948, 87-88. The board received his comments and took no action on them. The comments were released to the press on 1 Nov. 1948. See *Louisville Courier-Journal,* 14 Nov. 1948.

41. *Louisville Courier-Journal,* 14 Nov. 1948.

42. *Johnson v. Board of Trustees,* 25 Oct. 1948, 625 Civ. E.D. Ky. (1948), Order upon Pre-Trial Conference.

43. Ibid. More precisely, the order indicated that the only issues were "whether, in fact, the defendants have made adequate facilities and service within the State of Kentucky at the Kentucky State College for Negroes at Frankfort, Ky., for the education of the negro [sic] students in the professional and graduate field[s] involved in this action, and whether the provisions [were] alleged to have been constitutional requirements of equality, and whether any solely because of race can satisfy the Federal Constitutional requirements." *Johnson v. Board of Trustees,* 25 Oct. 1948, 625 Civ. E.D. Ky. (1948).

44. "Minutes of the Board of Education," 17 Dec. 1948, book 19, p. 92; 18 March 1949, book 19; 23 June 1949, book 20, p. 94; 24 March 1950, book 21, p. 193, KDLA.

45. *Johnson v. Board of Trustees,* 625 Civ. E.D. Ky. (1948), deposition of Thomas D. Clark and Maurice F. Seay, 15 March 1949.

46. John Hope Franklin to Robert L. Carter, 2, 11 April 1949; Thurgood Marshall to Goodwin Watson, 31 March 1949, NAACP Papers.

47. Thurgood Marshall to Goodwin Watson, 31 March 1949, NAACP Papers.

48. *Johnson v. Board of Trustees,* 27 April 1949.

49. Talbert, *University of Kentucky,* 175-76.

50. Ibid.

51. Ibid.

52. Preer, *Lawyers v. Educators,* 96.

53. "Biennial Report of the Superintendent," 40-43; "Biennial Report of the Superintendent of Public Instruction of the Commonwealth of Kentucky" (Frankfort: State Board of Education, 1941), 607-9.

54. Syvertsen, "Earle Chester Clements," 352-53.

55. Joseph S. Freeland to Thurgood Marshall, 15 Aug. 1949, NAACP Papers.

56. *Louisville Leader,* 4 Sept. 1948; *Baltimore Afro-American,* 4 Sept. 1948; *New York Times,* 2 Sept. 1948.

57. *Louisville Leader,* 12 Sept. 1948.

58. Ibid., 18 Dec. 1948; *Louisville Defender,* 8 July 1950.

59. *Louisville Leader,* 18 Dec. 1948.

60. Ibid., 21 May 1949.

61. L.T. Johnson, interview, 22 May 1984.
62. *Louisville Leader,* 23 July 1949; Hall, *The Rest of the Dream,* 158-62.
63. *Louisville Leader,* 23 July 1949.
64. University of Louisville Board of Trustees Minutes, 5 Oct. 1949, Univ. of Louisville Archives.
65. Wilson T. Wyatt, interview, 6 Sept. 1977, Univ. of Louisville Archives and Oral History.
66. L.T. Johnson, interview, 6 May 1976.
67. Wilson T. Wyatt, interview, 29 July 1976, Univ. of Louisville Archives and Oral History; *Louisville Defender,* 8 July 1950.
68. *Louisville Leader,* 5 Nov. 1949.
69. Ibid., 12 Nov. 1949.
70. L.T. Johnson, interview, 22 May 1984.
71. *New York Times,* 24 Aug. 1948.
72. Ibid.
73. *Pittsburgh Courier,* 21 Jan. 1950; *Chicago Defender,* 21 Jan. 1950.
74. *Chicago Defender,* 21 Jan. 1950; *Pittsburgh Courier,* 28 Jan. 1950.
75. Syvertsen, "Earle Chester Clements," 345.
76. O.C. Dawkins, "Kentucky Outgrows Segregation," *Survey* 86, no. 7 (July 1950): 358-59. Whites who had become dissatisfied with the Day Law included Barry Bingham, president of the Louisville Courier-Journal Publishing Company; Mark Ethridge, publisher of the *Courier-Journal,* and state representative James Hanratty, majority floor leader in the Kentucky House of Representatives. Hanratty's comments suggested a pragmatic white leadership: "Even if you don't like it [desegregation], it's the best thing that's coming" (359).
77. Harry Schacter, *Kentucky on the March* (New York: Harper and Brothers, 1949), 123-30. Schacter describes how Kentucky civic leaders from 1943 to the present defined Kentucky's problems for the remainder of the twentieth century. Summary reports of the committee were issued periodically throughout 1950. Each report, including one on education, argued that Kentucky's problems were large but solvable if the legislature, other constitutionally elected officials, and the voters agreed to make the necessary sacrifices. See *Reports of the Committee for Kentucky* (Louisville, n.p., 1950).
78. *Louisville Defender,* 14 Jan., 8 July 1950.
79. Acts of the General Assembly, 1950, chap. 155, pp. 615-16.
80. *Pittsburgh Courier,* 29 April 1950; *Chicago Defender,* 29 April 1950.
81. For a detailed study of the process, see Atwood, "The Public Negro College." The desegregation of Berea College occurred as the Berea Citizens Committee for the Repeal of the Day Law merged with the Berea

College Students for Democratic Actions. See Raymond Colley, "Day Law Amended," *Berea Alumnus* 20 (April 1950): 202-3.
    82. Atwood, "The Public Negro College," 354-58.
    83. Ibid. See also Jessie Parkhurst Guzman, *1952 Negro Yearbook* (New York: W.H. Wise, 1952), 239-41.
    84. Acts of the General Assembly, 1950, Senate Resolution 53, chap. 252, pp. 841-43. This resolution contained the Southern Regional Compact approved by the Kentucky legislature. Other states included in the compact were Florida, Maryland, Georgia, Louisiana, Alabama, Mississippi, Tennessee, Arkansas, Virginia, North Carolina, South Carolina, Texas, Oklahoma, and West Virginia. The compact began as an attempt to improve southern white higher education but became an important tool in collective resistance to desegregation. See U.S.Commission on Civil Rights, *Equal Protection,* 26-28.
    Kentucky blacks and racially moderate whites blunted the compact's segregation thrust with the enactment of Senate Resolution 62, Acts of the General Assembly, 1950, chap. 255, pp. 850-51. Specifically, the resolution ordered the state of Kentucky not to "erect, acquire, develop or maintain in any manner any educational institution within its borders to which Negroes will not be admitted on an equal basis with other races, nor shall any Negro citizen of Kentucky be forced to attend any segregated regional institution to obtain instruction in a particular course of study if there is in operation within the Commonwealth at the time an institution that offers the same course of study to students of other races" (851).
    85. *Pittsburgh Courier,* 10 June 1950.
    86. Atwood, "The Public Negro College," 357.
    87. For an extended discussion of the desegregation of the University of Louisville, see Hudson, "Louisville Municipal College," 76-107. See also G.D. Wilson, "Footprints in the Sand."
    Although this controversy did not impede University of Louisville desegregation, it reflected the caution expressed by contemporary black observers of desegregation efforts. See Oliver C. Cox, "Negro Teachers: Martyrs of Integration?" *Nation,* 25 April 1953, 347-48.
    88. Atwood, "The Public Negro College," 357.
    89. Under the 1936 Kentucky Government Reorganization Act, the Department of Finance received control over the University of Kentucky and the five state colleges, including Kentucky State. This control had political implications since the state Department of Finance came under the executive branch of the state government. Governors could affect college operations if it was politically expedient.
    In 1946 Gov. Simeon Willis allegedly used his influence in the selection of a new president of Morehead State Teachers College. Subsequently, the college lost its accreditation from the Southern Association of Colleges

and Secondary Schools. Other Kentucky schools were threatened with loss of accreditation if the political element in the presidential selection process was not removed. Following the election of Earle Clements as governor, the legislature decided in the next session to modify the state law permitting ouster of state college regents without cause. With this change, Morehead State regained its accreditation retroactively. Kentucky State, however, was excluded because its control came under the State Board of Education. See *Louisville Courier-Journal,* 2 Feb. 1952; Acts of the General Assembly, 1934, chap. 65, art. 4.

In 1950 the legislature created a statewide committee to "make a comprehensive study and survey of the requirements, needs and responsibilities of state government, . . . taking into consideration . . . the necessity of a balanced and coordinated program of government." The committee, composed of Democrats and Republicans, twenty-one whites and one black, sensed that the problems of public higher education were special. Hence, it contacted Earl J. McGrath, U.S. commissioner of education, to select a nonpartisan research survey team that would conduct an accurate and unbiased analysis. See John Dale Russell, ed., *Public Higher Education in Kentucky,* Legislative Research Commission, Frankfort, Ky., 31 January 1952, 1-185.

90. Acts of the General Assembly, 1952, chap. 41, pp. 67-75. Additionally, Lincoln Institute, which was deeded to the State Board of Education in 1947, became a part of Kentucky State and subject to its board of regents.

91. Atwood, "The Public Negro College," 354-56.

92. *Louisville Leader,* 5 Nov. 1949. Freeland also remained in contact with national NAACP assistant special counsel Robert L. Carter about the motions and progress of the case. See Robert L. Carter to Joseph S. Freeland, 8 Nov. 1949; Joseph S. Freeland to Robert L. Carter, 3 Feb. 1950, NAACP Papers.

93. Acts of the General Assembly, 1938, chap. 29, pp. 1082-91.

94. *Wilson et. al. v. City of Paducah et. al.,* Civ. No. 616, W.D. Ky. (1951), summary judgment, 27 Oct. 1950.

95. *Louisville Courier-Journal,* 4 Dec. 1953; Glen Murrell, "The Desegregation of Paducah Junior College," *Register of the Kentucky Historical Society* 67 (Jan. 1969): 63-79.

96. *Wilson v. City of Paducah,* 100 F. Supp. 116 W.D. Ky. (1951), p. 117.

97. *Louisville Courier-Journal,* 4 Dec. 1953.

98. *Journal of the Senate,* 1954, 6 Jan. 1954, 26-31.

99. Wendell P. Butler, ed., "History of Education in Kentucky, 1939-1964," *Commonwealth of Kentucky Educational Bulletin* 31, no. 4 (Nov. 1963): 135-36.

100. Ibid., 138.

101. *Brown v. Board of Education,* 347 U.S. 497 (1956). The four cases involved in the Brown decision were *Brown v. Board of Education of Topeka, Kansas,* 98 F. Supp. 797 (D. Kan.); *Briggs v. Elliot,* 98 F. Supp. 529 E.D. S.C. (1951); *Davis v. County School Board,* 103 F. Supp. 337 E.D. Va. (1952); and *Gebhart v. Belton,* 87 A. 2d. 862 Del. Ch. (1952).

102. *Kentucky's Black Heritage,* (Frankfort: Kentucky Commission on Human Rights, 1971), 103. Wetherby remarked, "Kentucky will do whatever is necessary to comply with the law."

103. *Omaha Star,* 9 July 1954.

104. *Chicago Defender,* 17 July 1954.

105. *Louisville Courier-Journal,* 3 July, 14 Nov. 1954, 24 June 1955; John E. Kleber, "As Luck Would Have It; An Overview of Lawrence W. Wetherby as Governor, 1950-1955," *Register of the Kentucky Historical Society* 84, no. 4 (autumn 1986): 415-16.

106. *Kentucky's Black Heritage,* 104.

107. *Louisville Courier-Journal,* 30 Sept. 1954. At the same time, Kentucky State employed one white faculty member and a white school physician. Despite this minimal white faculty presence, Ogden decided to withdraw a week later. The *Louisville Courier-Journal* devoted one paragraph to her withdrawal (7 Oct. 1954).

108. R.B. Atwood, "Kentucky State College and Integration," *Kentucky Teachers Association Journal* 1 (Oct.-Nov. 1954): 10-13.

109. *New York Times,* 6 May 1956, 74.

110. *Willis v. Walker,* 136 F. Supp. 177, 181 (1955). This case included an admission by Adair County Schools that segregation by race was illegal.

111. Guzman, *1952 Negro Yearbook,* 239. The Kentucky colleges and universities that admitted blacks in the fall of 1950 and the numbers of blacks admitted were Bellarmine College (3), Berea College (2), Louisville Presbyterian Seminary (1), Nazareth Women's College (4), University of Kentucky summer term of 1949 (31), University of Louisville (5) and Ursuline College (3). Other state colleges outside of Kentucky State refused admittance to blacks as a matter of policy based on the Day Law.

112. Charles H. Parrish, Jr. "Desegregated Higher Education in Kentucky," *Journal of Negro Education* 27 (1958): 260-68. Parrish's study revealed that by 1958 Morehead State College had admitted 4 and Eastern Kentucky State College had admitted 3. The University of Louisville estimated that 125 blacks had been enrolled; 185 had matriculated at the University of Kentucky.

113. Roscoe Griffen, *A Tentative Description and Analysis of the School Desegregation Crisis in Sturgis, Kentucky, August 31-September 19, 1956* (New York: Anti-Defamation League of B'nai B'rith, 1956); *New York Times,* 11 Sept. 1956; Bullock, Negro Education in the South, 252-53.

114. Omer Carmichael and James Weldon, *The Louisville Story* (New York: Simon and Schuster, 1957); "Is 'Voluntary' Integration the Answer?" *U.S. News and World Report*, 5 Oct. 1956, 46-56, 142-49.

115. *Florida ex rel. Hawkins v. Board of Control*, 350 U.S. 413 (1956). Ironically, Virgil Hawkins did not receive "prompt admission" because he failed to score the required 340 on the University of Florida Law School's admission test.

116. W.F. O'Donnell to R.B. Atwood, 26 April 1955, box 178, Papers. Atwood's response to President O'Donnell of Eastern Kentucky State College included the following: "My own belief is that at some date in the not too distant future the state supported institutions should open their doors to persons regardless of race. We, of course, realize that Kentucky State will no longer have a captive student body such as it had under segregation." See R.B. Atwood to W.F. O'Donnell, 6 May 1955, box 178, Martin Papers.

For the role of President Kelly Thompson of Western Kentucky State College, see Lowell H. Harrison, *Western Kentucky University* (Lexington: Univ. Press of Kentucky, 1987), 145.

117. Morehead State's contribution to this process is discussed in Harry Eugene Rose, "The Historical Development of a State College: Morehead Kentucky State College, 1887-1964" (Ed.D. diss., Univ. of Cincinnati, 1965), 375. Rose implied but did not clearly state that Morehead was the first white state-supported college to admit blacks to classes and to its dormitories. According to Rose's 1965 interview with Pres. Adron Doran, the college was the first in the Ohio Valley Conference to have black members of its varsity teams, and thus it signaled an end to black exclusion in a regional sports conference (376).

118. Dickey, interview.

119. Statistics on pre-desegregation enrollments are uneven at best. Sources for such data are the Minutes of the State Board of Education, books 5-25; reports of Kentucky State presidents under its various institutional names from 1887-1934, i.e., State Normal School for Colored Persons, Kentucky Normal and Industrial Institute for Colored Persons, and Kentucky State Industrial College for Colored Persons; the Legislative Research Commission; and J.D. Russell, *Public Higher Education in Kentucky*, 17. According to these combined sources, Kentucky State's average enrollment from 1904 to 1954 was 500. Although it declined to 530 (1956-57) from 716 (1949-50), this number corresponded to the overall average.

The publicity surrounding the Ogden case did not produce subsequent white enrollments, but white students gradually found the campus in small numbers. By 1958 Charles H. Parrish Jr. reported that Kentucky State had an enrollment of 53 whites. See Parrish, "Desegregated Higher Education in Kentucky," 265.

120. The origins of the desegregated mission for Kentucky State were well publicized. President Atwood served as its chief advocate. See Atwood, "Kentucky State College," 9-11; *Louisville Buyers Guide and News Digest* 2 (July 1956): 6, 14; *Louisville Courier Journal,* 19 July 1959. The college used a study by a white university consultant to defend this position See W. Scott Hall, "Kentucky State College of the Future: An Initial Study," 1958, typescript, KSU-BLA.

Epilogue

1. Gerald Smith, "Student Demonstrations and the Dilemma of the Black College President in 1960: Rufus Atwood and Kentucky State College," *Register of the Kentucky Historical Society* 88, no. 3 (summer 1990): 318-34. See also *Louisville Defender,* 8, 15 March, 19 April, 7 June 1962; *New York Times,* 11 Sept. 1962.

2. See Ann Jackson Heartwell-Hunter, *Against the Tide* (Lexington: Published by the author, 1987). Hunter served as dean of students from 1947 to 1965 and supported Atwood during a crucial period in Kentucky State's history. Until the 1960 student upheavals, the campus newspaper, *Kentucky Thorobred,* expressed a pro-administration view. See *Kentucky Thorobred,* vols. 2-29, KSU-BLA. For a complete biography of Atwood's accomplishments at Kentucky State, see G.L. Smith, *A Black Educator,* 35-182.

3. *Kentucky's Black Heritage,* 140.

4. "Minority Affairs Celebrates 20 Years on Campus," *Communi-K* [Univ. of Kentucky faculty/staff newspaper], 31 Oct. 1991; *Kentucky's Black Heritage,* 139-40.

5. Michael Washington, "The Quest for Inclusion: The Struggle of Black Students and the Afro-American Studies Program at Northern Kentucky University," *Journal of Kentucky Studies* 10 (Sept. 1993): 91-104.

6. The debate over Kentucky State's continuance began in 1962 following the student upheavals and dismissals. The following articles describe public events and commentary in 1962-63: *Louisville Defender,* 8, 15 March, 19 April, 7 June 1962; *New York Times,* 11 Sept. 1962. An extensive review of Kentucky State's prospects can be found in M.M. Chambers, Thomas Pullen, and Broadus E. Sawyer, *The Future of Kentucky State College* (Frankfort: Kentucky Council on Public Higher Education, 1962), 1-40.

7. *Louisville Courier-Journal,* 6 Oct. 1963, 22 Feb., 5, 29, 30 April, 1 May 1968.

8. The litigation that originally started this process can be found in *Adams v. Richardson,* 480 F.2d 1159 D.C. Circ. (1973). Other cases relative to this process are *Geier v. Blanton,* 427 F. Supp. 644 (M.D. Tenn. 1977), and *Geier v. Tennessee,* 597 F. 2d 1056 6th Cir. (1979), *cert. denied,* 444 U.S. 886

(1979). For the formal notice of the review of Kentucky higher education institutions by the U.S. Department of Education, see William H. Thomas, U.S. Department of Education, to Gov. John Y. Brown Jr., 15 Jan. 1981, author's copy.

9. "Kentucky's Plan in Response to the Office of Civil Rights Letter of January 15, 1981," Jan. 1982, Kentucky Council on Higher Education, Frankfort. See also *Chronicle on Higher Education,* 24 Nov. 1982.

10. As early as 1975, Kentucky State University alumni began to express concern about the attacks on the institution and its leaders. See "The Situation at Kentucky State," *American Baptist,* 3 Jan. 1975; *Louisville Courier-Journal,* 2 Feb. 1975. In 1980 the Kentucky State alumni association and the NAACP state conference were becoming involved in the controversy. See *Louisville Courier-Journal,* 5 Aug. 1980.

11. Interview with Lyman Johnson and Raymond Burse on "Emphasis," 21 Nov. 1981, WAVE-TV, Louisville; *Louisville Courier-Journal,* 10 June 1981.

12. *Frankfort State Journal,* 4 Aug. 1980, *Louisville Courier-Journal,* 7 Aug. 1980, 22 Feb., 16 March 1982. See also "Kentucky's Plan in Response to the Office of Civil Rights Letter of January 15, 1981-January 1982" *Council Report—Kentucky Council on Higher Education,* March 1982 Frankfort, S1-S7.

13. "President's Report, Kentucky State University, December 1, 1975–June 30, 1978," Frankfort. Press reports for the early years of the Butts era focus on out-of-state enrollment and on-campus crime issues but fail to editorialize the positive achievements, such as the $406,000 grant from the Kellogg Foundation for the School of Business. In April 1978 the Kentucky State University Alumni Association condemned the white media for their unfair treatment of the university. See *Louisville Defender,* 27 April 1978.

14. *Louisville Courier-Journal,* 22 Feb., 11, 16 March 1982.

15. *Frankfort State Journal,* 17 Aug., 21 Sept. 1983.

16. *Louisville Courier-Journal,* 25 March 1989; *KSU Magazine* 7, no. 2 (summer 1989): 14.

17. *Louisville Courier-Journal,* 18 Sept. 1991; *Frankfort State Journal,* 17 Sept. 1991.

18. *Louisville Courier Journal,* 24, 26, 28 Sept., 2 Oct. 1991.

19. *Louisville Courier-Journal,* 19 Oct., 6 Dec. 1991.

20. *Louisville Courier-Journal,* 31 Oct. 1991.

Bibliography

Abbreviations Employed in the Notes and the Bibliography

KDLA   Kentucky Department for Libraries and Archives, Frankfort, Ky.
KSU-BLA   Kentucky State University Blazer Library Archives
NAACP Papers NAACP Papers, Manuscript Division, Library of Congress
SBCR   Simmons Bible College Records
SPI-KDLA   "Biennial Report of the Superintendents of Public Instruction," Kentucky Department for Libraries and Archives Superintendent's MSS. Superintendent of Public Instruction Collection. Kentucky Department of Libraries and Archives, Frankfort, Ky.

Bibliographical and Research Aids

Chambers, Frederick. *Black Higher Education in the United States.* Westport, Conn.: Greenwood Press, 1978.

Coleman, Winston. *A Bibliography of Kentucky History.* Lexington: Univ. of Kentucky Press, 1949.

Field Services Office of Kentucky Historical Society. *Directory of Kentucky History Organizations.* Frankfort, Ky., 1982.

Hardin, Bayless. "Frankfort, Kentucky Newspapers." *Register of the Kentucky Historical Society* 39 (Oct. 1941): 392-99.

Hinds, Charles F. "Public Records Management in Kentucky." *Register of the Kentucky Historical Society* 55 (July 1957): 291-292.

———. "Kentucky Records: How to Use Them and Where They Are." *National Genealogical Society Quarterly* 59 (March 1971): 3-7.

———. *First Annual Kentucky Seminar—1974.* Frankfort: Kentucky Genealogical Society, 1974.

Jillson, Willard Rouse. *An Historical Bibliography of Frankfort.* Frankfort, Ky.: State Journal Co., 1942.

160   Bibliography

Kleber, John, ed. *The Kentucky Encyclopedia.* Lexington: Univ. Press of Kentucky, 1992.

Louisville Courier-Journal. Microfilm Index, 1917-1977. Frankfort: Kentucky Department of Libraries and Archives, n.d.

Pride, Armistead S. *Negro Newspapers on Microfilm.* Washington, D.C.: Library of Congress Photoduplication Division, 1953.

Social Science Institute of Fisk University. *Sociology of the South: A Bibliography and Critique of Doctoral Dissertations and Masters Theses Written on Aspects of the South.* Nashville, Tenn.: Fisk Univ., 1951.

Toppin, Edgar A. *A Biographical History of Blacks in America Since 1528.* New York: David McKay, 1971.

Public Documents

Acts of the General Assembly of the Commonwealth of Kentucky.

Kentucky House of Representatives. *Journal of the House of Representatives of the Commonwealth of Kentucky.*

Kentucky Senate. *Journal of the Senate of the Commonwealth of Kentucky.*

Kentucky State Board of Education. *Minutes of the State Board of Education of the Commonwealth of Kentucky.*

Tape Recorded Interviews

Alumni Faculty Oral History Project interviews below are in the Department of Special Collections and Archives, University of Kentucky.

Clark, Thomas D. 14 June 1978.

Dickey, Frank G. 2 Feb. 1977.

Eaton, W. Clement. 5 Nov. 1975.

Galloway, Oscar. 17 Sept. 1976.

Nutter, Homer. 11 June 1978.

Oberst, Paul. 22 Aug. 1978.

Tape recorded interviews listed below are available at the University of Louisville Archives.

Alexander, Lloyd, 7 June 1977.

Bottoms, Jesse V. 15 Dec. 1977.

Butler, Henrietta. 4 Jan. 1978.

Cole, C. Lattimore. 11 Nov. 1977.

Ealy, William J. 5 Aug. 1977.
Holmes, W.L. 5 Aug. 1977.
Johnson, Lyman T. 29 June 1963, 6 May 1976.
Parrish, Charles H. 20 Nov. 1974, 1 Dec. 1976, 2 Feb. 1977, 16 March 1977.
Perry, William H. 9 Sept. 1977.
Stanley, Kenneth. 12 May 1977.
Tape Recordings of these interviews are in the author's possession.
Chandler, Albert B. 21 May 1984.
Dailey, Catherine B. 12 Jan. 1983.
Johnson, Lyman T. 22 May 1984.
Raines, Eugene D. 3 Jan. 1983.
Wright, Arnold W. 3 March 1983.

Manuscripts

Ashcraft, J.N. "Audit July 1, 1925 to December, 1928—Report of Investigation of the Management of the Affairs of the Kentucky Normal and Industrial Institute and Audit by W. M. Van House, Asst. Inspector and Examiner." 11 Feb. 1929. Superintendent's MSS.
———. "Suggestions as to the Best Methods to Follow in Placing the Above Institutions on a Business Basis." 14 March 1929. Superintendent's MSS.
Atwood, Rufus Ballard. Papers. KSU-BLA.
Burch, E.R. "Salaries Paid in Fiscal Year Ended June 30, 1928 and by Kentucky Normal and Industrial College. Frankfort, KY." 11 Sept. 1928. Superintendent's MSS.
———. "Report for KY. Normal and Industrial College, Frankfort, KY." Vols. A and B. 15 Nov. 1928. Superintendent's MSS.
Chandler, Albert Benjamin. Papers. Special Collections, Margaret I. King Library, Univ. of Kentucky.
Clements, Earle Chester. Papers. Special Collections, Margaret I. King Library, Univ. of Kentucky.
Council of Cooperative College Projects. "Minutes January 1, 1956 to March 4, 1963." KSU-BLA.
Day Law Files. Berea College Archives.
Donovan, Herman Lee. Papers. Eastern Kentucky Univ. Library Archives.
Griffenhagen and Associates. "Report on the Audit and Budget Survey of Kentucky State Industrial College for Colored Persons." 15 Jan. 1934. KDLA.

Johnson, Keen. Papers. Eastern Kentucky Univ. Archives.

Kappa Alpha Psi Fraternity Inc. Alpha Upsilon Chapter. "Biographical Sketches of Kentucky State Industrial College Presidents. 1887-1937." 29 April 1937.

Kentucky Normal and Industrial College. "Financial Records 1926-1928." Superintendent's MSS.

Kentucky Normal and Industrial Institute for Colored Persons. "Minutes of the Board of Trustees, Financial Records and Letters. 1914-1929." Superintendent's MSS.

————. "Audit Reports and Special Reports, 1922-1930." Superintendent's MSS.

Kentucky State Board of Education. "Minutes of the State Board of Education." Vols. 5-25. 1934-52, KDLA.

Kentucky State College. "Lyceum Committee Minutes, November 17, 1930 thru October 19, 1948." KSU-BLA.

————. "Minutes of the Executive Council, May 1, 1969 to October 24, 1974." KSU-BLA.

Kentucky State College for Negroes. "Minutes of Faculty and Executive Council. November 1929-November 17, 1941." KSU-BLA.

Kentucky State Normal School for Colored Persons. "Examination Book—1893." Superintendent's MSS.

————. "Faculty Meetings State Normal School, September 1897 through May 1911." KSU-BLA.

Lincoln Institute. "Articles of Incorporation." Superintendent's MSS.

Lincoln Institute Scrapbooks. Univ. of Louisville Archives.

Louisville Municipal College for Negroes. President's Office Files. 1924-54. Univ. of Louisville Archives.

Martin, Robert F. Papers. Eastern Kentucky Univ. Archives.

Mayes, T. Scott. State Inspector and Examiner. "Detailed Audit of Receipts and Disbursements and the General Management of the Kentucky Normal and Industrial Institute for Colored Persons located at Frankfort, KY." 8 Oct. 1925. Superintendent's MSS.

Minute Book 1916 of Kentucky Negro Exposition Co. (also contains Faculty Minutes of Kentucky Normal and Industrial Institute, 10 Jan. 1923 to 4 June 1928). KSU-BLA.

"Minutes of the Executive Council and Faculty of Kentucky State Univ., November 18, 1954-November 7, 1960." KSU-BLA.

National Association for the Advancement of Colored People. Papers. Manuscript Division, Library of Congress.

National Urban League. Papers. Manuscript Division, Library of Congress.

Parrish, Charles Henry, Jr. Papers. Univ. of Louisville Archives.

Peat, Marwick, Mitchell and Company. "Kentucky State Industrial College for Colored Persons—Report on Audit of Accounts for the Two Years Ended June 30, 1930." 18 Sept. 1930. Superintendent's MSS.

Russell, Green Pinckney. "Adjustments Suggested in Accountants Report." 10 Dec. 1928. Superintendent's MSS.

Sewell, Nat B. "Report of Nat B. Sewell, State Inspector and Examiner upon an Investigation of the Accounts, Management, and Affairs of Kentucky State Industrial College for Colored Persons. Frankfort, Kentucky, July 29, 1932." KSU-BLA.

Simmons Bible College. "Simmons Bible College Records, 1869-1971." Univ. of Louisville Archives.

Spingarn, Arthur Barnett. Papers. Manuscript Division, Library of Congress.

Washington, Booker Taliferro. Papers. Manuscript Division, Library of Congress.

West Kentucky Industrial College. "Minutes of the Board of Trustees, 1924-1934." Superintendent's MSS.

Wetherby, Lawrence W. Papers. Special Collections, Univ. of Kentucky Library.

Willis, Simeon. Papers. Special Collections, Univ. of Kentucky Library.

Willson, Augustus E. Papers. Filson Club Archives. Louisville, Ky.

Wilson, George Dewey. "Footprints in the Sand—Kentucky Sand." 1982. KSU-BLA.

———. Papers. Univ. of Louisville Archives.

Woodson, Carter Goodwin. Papers. Manuscript Division, Library of Congress.

Young, Whitney M., Sr. Papers. KSU-BLA.

Pamphlets

Bullitt County 175th Centennial Committee (1797-1971). Sheperdsville, Ky., 1971.

Curry, J.L.M. *Education of the Negro since 1860*. Baltimore, 1894.

Louisville Municipal College. *Bulletins*. 1931-51. Univ. of Louisville Archives.

Obsequies for Dr. Dennis Henry Anderson. Clarence L. Timberlake Papers. Murray State Univ. Archives.

Simmons University. *Simmons University: Past and Present Souvenir Yearbook*. 1964. Univ. of Louisville Archives.

Timberlake, Clarence L. *Politics and the Schools.* Frankfort, Ky. Clarence L. Timberlake Papers, Murray State Univ. Archives.

West Kentucky Vocational School. *Door to Industrial Opportunity.* Clarence L. Timberlake Papers, Murray State Univ. Archives.

Books

Allen, James Lane. *The Bluegrass Region of Kentucky.* New York: Macmillan, 1892.

Aptheker, Herbert, ed. *W.E.B. Du Bois: The Education of Black People, Ten Critiques 1906-1960.* Amherst: Univ. of Massachusetts Press, 1982.

Ashmore, Harry S. *The Negro and the Schools.* Chapel Hill: Univ. of North Carolina Press, 1954.

Bailyn, Bernard. *Education in the Forming of American Society.* New York: Vintage Press, 1960.

Blaustein, Albert P., and Clarence Clyde Ferguson Jr. *Desegregation and the Law.* New Brunswick, N.J.: Rutgers Univ. Press, 1957.

Bond, Horace Mann. *Negro Education in Alabama: A Study in Cotton and Steel.* Washington, D.C.: Associated Publishers, 1939.

Bowles, Frank, and Frank A. Decosta. *Between Two Worlds.* New York: McGraw-Hill, 1971.

Brubacher, John S., and Rudy Willis. *Higher Education in Transition: A History of American Colleges and Universities.* New York: Harper and Row, 1968.

Bullock, Henry Allen. *A History of Negro Education in the South.* New York: Praeger, 1970.

Cable, George Washington, *The Negro Question.* Garden City, N.Y.: Doubleday, 1953.

Chandler, David Leon. *The Binghams of Louisville.* New York: Crown Publishing, 1987.

Clement, Rufus Early. *The Impact of the War upon Negro Graduate and Professional Schools.* Washington, D.C.: Howard Univ. Press, 1942.

Clift, Virgil, Archibald Anderson, and H. Gordon Hullfish, eds. *Negro Education in America.* New York: Harper Brothers, 1962.

Collins, Lewis, and Richard H. Collins. *History of Kentucky.* 2 vols. 1874 edition. Berea, Ky.: Kentucke Imprints, 1974.

Cross, George Lynn. *Blacks in White Colleges: Oklahoma's Landmark Cases.* Norman: Univ. of Oklahoma Press, 1975.

Curry, Richard O. *Radicalism, Racism and Party Alignment: The Border*

States during Reconstruction. Baltimore: John Hopkins Univ. Press, 1969.

Dawson, Osceola Aleese. *The Timberlake Story.* Carbondale, Ill.: Dunaway-Sinclair, 1959.

Drake, Mrs. William Preston, et. al. *Kentucky in Retrospect, 1792-1967.* Frankfort: Kentucky Historical Society, 1967.

Du Bois, William Edward Burghardt. *The College Bred Negro American.* Atlanta: Atlanta Univ. Press, 1910.

Dunnigan, Alice Allison. *The Fascinating Story of Black Kentuckians.* Washington, D.C.: Associated Publishers, 1982.

Egerton, John. *The Black Public Colleges.* Nashville, Tenn.: Race Relations Information Center, 1971.

Fee, John Gregg. *Autobiography.* Chicago: National Christian Association, 1891.

Fenton, John. *Politics in the Border States.* New Orleans: Hauser Press, 1957.

Flexner, Abraham. *Medical Education in the United States and Canada.* New York: Carnegie Foundation for the Advancement of Teaching, 1910.

From Servitude to Service. Boston: American Unitarian Association, 1905.

Gallagher, Buell Gordon. *American Caste and the Negro College.* New York: Gordian Press, 1966.

General Association of Colored Baptists in Kentucky. *Golden Jubilee of the General Association of Colored Baptists in Kentucky.* Louisville: Mayes Printing, 1915.

————. *Diamond Jubilee of the General Association of Colored Baptists in Kentucky.* Louisville: American Baptist Press, 1943.

Gibson, William H. *Historical Sketch of the Progress of the Colored Race in Louisville, Kentucky.* Louisville: Bradley and Gilbert, 1897.

Goode, Cecil E., and Woodford L. Gardner Jr. *Barren County Heritage.* Bowling Green, Ky.: Homestead Press, 1980.

Green, Elisha W. *Life of Rev. Elisha Green, One of the Founders of Kentucky Normal and Theological Institute.* Maysville, Ky.: Republican Printing, 1888.

Hall, Wade. *The Rest of the Dream: The Black Odyssey of Lyman Johnson.* Lexington: Univ. Press of Kentucky, 1989.

Hampton, George A. *History of the General Association of Colored Baptists in Kentucky: Centennial Volume (1868-1968).* Louisville: General Association of Baptists in Kentucky, 1970.

Hardin, John A. *Onward and Upward: A Centennial History of Kentucky State University, 1886-1986*. Frankfort: Kentucky State Univ., 1987.

Holmes, Dwight Oliver Wendell. *The Evolution of the Negro College*. New York: Teachers College Press, 1934.

Hopkins, James F. *The University of Kentucky: Origins and Early Years*. Lexington: Univ. of Kentucky Press, 1951.

Horton, John Benjamin. *Not without Struggle*. New York: Vantage Press, 1979.

————. *Old War Horse of Kentucky*. Louisville: J. Benjamin Horton, 1986.

Jencks, Christopher, and David Riesman. *The Academic Revolution*. Garden City, N.Y.: Doubleday, 1968.

Jewell, Malcolm, and Everett W. Cunningham. *Kentucky Politics*. Lexington: Univ. of Kentucky Press, 1968.

Johnson, Charles Spurgeon. *The Negro College Graduate*. Chapel Hill: Univ. of North Carolina Press, 1938.

Johnson, William Decker. *Biographical Sketches of Prominent Negro Men and Women*. Lexington, Ky.: Standard Print, 1897.

Jones, Paul William Lawless. *A History of KY. Normal and Industrial Institute*. Frankfort, Ky.: Published by the author, 1912.

Kerns, J. Harvey, ed. *A Survey of the Economic and Cultural Conditions of the Negro Population of Louisville, KY*. New York: National Urban League, 1948.

Klotter, James C. *William Goebel: Politics of Wrath*. Lexington: Univ. of Kentucky Press, 1977.

Kluger, Richard, *Simple Justice*. New York: Alfred A. Knopf, 1975.

Lamon, Lester C. *Black Tennesseans, 1900-1930*. Knoxville: Univ. of Tennessee Press, 1977.

Leavell, Ullin Whitney. *Philanthropy in Negro Education*. Nashville, Tenn.: George Peabody College, 1930.

LeMelle, Tilden, and Wilbert LeMelle. *The Black College: Strategy for Relevancy*. New York: Praeger, 1969.

Logan, Rayford. *Howard University: The First Hundred Years*. New York: New York Univ. Press, 1975.

Louisville, University of. *A Century of Municipal Higher Education*. Chicago: Lincoln Printing, 1937.

————. *A Centennial History of the University of Louisville*. Louisville: Univ. of Louisville, 1939.

Lucas, Marion B. *A History of Blacks in Kentucky*. Vol. 1, *From Slavery to Segregation, 1760-1891*. Frankfort: Kentucky Historical Society, 1992.

Marrs, Elijah P. *Life and History of Rev. Elijah P. Marrs*. Louisville: Bradley and Gilbert, 1885.

McCuistion, Fred. *Higher Education of Negroes: Summary*. Nashville, Tenn.: Southern Association of Colleges and Secondary Schools, 1933.

McGrath, Earl James. *The Predominantly Negro Colleges and Universities in Transition*. New York: Teachers College, Columbia Univ. 1965.

McVey, Frank L. *The Gates Open Slowly: A History of Education in Kentucky*. Lexington: Univ. of Kentucky Press, 1949.

Moore, Jesse T. *A Search for Equality: The National Urban League, 1910-1961*. University Park, Pa.: Pennsylvania State Univ. Press, 1981.

National Advisory Committee on Black Higher Education and Black Colleges and Universities. *Black Colleges and Universities: An Essential Component of a Diverse System of Higher Education*. Washington, D.C.: Department of Health, Education, and Welfare, 1979.

Peck, Elizabeth Sinclair. *Berea's First Century*. Lexington: Univ. of Kentucky Press, 1955.

Perrin, William Henry. ed. *(History of the) County of Trigg Kentucky*. Chicago: F.A. Battey, 1884.

Pierce, Neal R. *The Border States South*. New York: Macmillan, 1975.

Powell, Jacob Wesley. *Bird's Eye View of the General Conference of the African Methodist Episcopal Zion Church*. Boston: Lavalle Press, 1918.

Preer, Jean L. *Lawyers v. Educators: Black Colleges and Desegregation in Public Higher Education*. Westport, Conn.: Greenwood Press, 1982.

Roland, Charles P. *The Improbable Era: The South since World War II*. Lexington: Univ. of Kentucky Press, 1975.

Rudolph, Frederick. *The American College and University*. New York: Alfred A. Knopf, 1968.

Scott, William J. *Negro Students and Their Colleges*. Boston: Meador, 1949.

Sears, Richard D. *"A Practical Recognition of the Brotherhood of Man": John G. Fee and the Camp Nelson Experience*. Berea, Ky.: Berea College Press, 1986.

Simmons, William J. *Men of Mark: Eminent, Progressive and Rising*. Cleveland, 1886; reprint, New York: Arno Press, 1979.

Smith, Gerald L. *A Black Educator in the Segregated South: Kentucky's Rufus B. Atwood*. Lexington: Univ. Press of Kentucky, 1994.

Smith, Leslie Shively. *Around Muhlenberg County, Kentucky: A Black History.* Evansville, Ind.: Unigraphic, 1979.

Stokes, Anson Phelps. *Progress in Negro Status and Race Relations, 1911-1946: The Thirty-Five Year Report of the Phelps-Stokes Fund Inc.* New York: Phelps-Stokes Fund, 1948.

Talbert, Charles Gano, *University of Kentucky: The Maturing Years.* Lexington: Univ. of Kentucky Press, 1965.

Thomas, Samuel N. *Louisville: Since the Twenties.* Louisville: *Louisville Courier-Journal* and *Louisville Times Press,* 1961.

Thorpe, Earl. *The Mind of the Negro: An Intellectual History of the Afro-Americans.* Baton Rouge, La.: Ortlieb Press, 1961.

U.S. Commission on Civil Rights. *Equal Protection of the Laws in Public Higher Education.* Washington: Government Printing Office, 1960.

————. *The Black/White Colleges: Dismantling the Dual System of Higher Education.* Clearinghouse Publication 66. Washington, D.C.: U.S. Government Printing Office, 1981.

Wasby, Stephen L., and Rosemary Metrailer. *Desegregation from Brown to Alexander.* Carbondale: Southern Illinois Univ. Press, 1977.

Weiss, Nancy J. *The National Urban League, 1910-1940.* New York: Oxford Univ. Press, 1974.

Wilkinson, J. Harvie, III. *From Brown to Bakke.* Fairlawn, N.J.: Oxford Univ. Press, 1979.

Williams, Lawrence H. *Black Higher Education in Kentucky, 1879-1930: The History of Simmons University.* Lewiston, N.Y.: Edward Mellen Press, 1987.

Williams, Roger M. *The Bonds: An American Family.* New York: Athenaeum, 1971.

Willis, George L., Sr., ed. *History of Shelby County, Kentucky.* Louisville: Shelby County Genealogical Society's Committee on Printing, 1929.

Wolters, Raymond. *The New Negro on Campus: Black College Rebellions of the 1920s.* Princeton, N.J.: Princeton Univ. Press, 1977.

Woodson, Carter G. *Miseducation of the Negro.* Washington, D.C.: Associated Publishers, 1938.

Woofter, T.J., Jr. *Negro Problems in Cities.* New York: Doubleday, Doran, 1928.

Wright, Arthur D. *The Negro Rural School Fund, Inc. of the Anna T. Jeanes Foundation.* New York: Negro Rural School Fund, 1933.

Wright, George C. *Life behind a Veil.* Baton Rouge: Louisiana State Univ. Press, 1985.

————. *A History of Blacks in Kentucky.* Vol. 2, *In Pursuit of Equality, 1890-1980.* Frankfort: Kentucky Historical Society, 1992.

Yater, George H. *Two Hundred Years at the Falls of the Ohio.* Louisville: Heritage Corporation, 1979.

Young, Bennett. *History of Jessamine County.* Louisville: Courier-Journal Job Printing, 1898.

Articles

Allen, Leroy. "The Possibilities of Integration for Public Colleges Founded for Negroes." *Journal of Negro Education* 35 (fall 1966): 452-61.

Atwood, Rufus Ballard. "The Role of Negro Higher Education in Post War Reconstruction: The Negro Land Grant College." *Journal of Negro Education* 11 (July 1942): 391-95.

————. "The Public Negro College in a Racially Integrated System of Higher Education" *Journal of Negro Education* 21 (summer 1952): 352-63.

————. "President of Kentucky State College Considers Integration Opportunity for Growth." *Louisville Buyers Guide and New Digest* 2 (July 1956): 6, 14.

Badger, Henry G. "Colleges That Did Not Survive." *Journal of Negro Education* 35 (fall 1966): 306-12.

Belles, A. Gilbert. "The College Faculty, the Negro Scholar, and the Julius Rosenwald Fund." *Journal of Negro History* 54 (Oct. 1969): 383-92.

"Black Politics in Kentucky." *Crisis* 19, no. 3 (Jan. 1920): 149.

Bond, Horace Mann. "The Origin and Development of the Negro Church Related College." *Journal of Negro Education* 29 (summer 1969): 217.

Branson, Herman. "The Role of the Negro College in the Preparation of Technical Personnel for the War Effort." *Journal of Negro Education* 11 (July 1942): 297-355.

Brewer, William. Review of *Survey of Negro Colleges and Universities,* edited by Arthur Klein. *Journal of Negro History* 14 (July 1929): 355.

Brown, Thomas J. "The Roots of Bluegrass Insurgency: An Analysis of the Populist Movement in Kentucky." *Register of the Kentucky Historical Society* 78 (fall 1980): 219-42.

Burnside, Jacqueline G. "Suspicion versus Faith: Negro Criticisms of Berea College in the Nineteenth Century." *Register of the Kentucky History Society* 83, no. 3 (summer 1985): 237-66.

Hardin, John A. "Green Pinckney Russell, Francis Marion Wood and Kentucky Normal and Industrial Institute, 1912-1929: A Study in Politics and Race," *Filson Club History Quarterly* 68, no. 2 (April 1995): 171-88.

Heckman, Richard, and Betty Jean Hall. "Berea College and the Day Law." *Register of the Kentucky Historical Society* 66 (Jan. 1968): 35-52.

Holmes, Dwight Oliver Wendell. "The Negro College Faces the Depression." *Journal of Negro Education* 2 (Jan. 1933): 16-24.

Horton, John Benjamin. "Selected Biographical Sketches." *Kentucky Negro Journal* (Dec. 1958): 79-107.

———. "Charles W. Anderson: The Measure of the Man." *Kentucky Negro Journal* 3, no. 3 (1960): 8.

Jencks, Christopher, and David Reisman. "The American Negro College." *Harvard Educational Review* 37 (winter 1967): 3-60.

Jenkins, Martin D. "The Future of the Desegregated Negro College: A Critical Summary." *Journal of Negro Education* 27 (summer 1958): 419-29.

Johnson, Guy B. "Desegregation and the Future of the Negro College: A Critical Summary." *Journal of Negro Education* 27 (summer 1958): 430-35.

Jones, Mack. "Responsibility of the Black College to the Black Community." *Daedalus* 100 (summer 1971): 732-44.

Kent, Raymond Asa. "A Municipal College of Liberal Arts." *Opportunity* 20 (Feb. 1942): 42-43.

Kousser, J. Morgan. "Making Separate Equal: Integration of Black and White School Funds in Kentucky." *Journal of Interdisciplinary History* 10 (winter 1980): 399-428.

Lane, David A., Jr. "The Junior College Movement among Negroes." *Journal of Negro Education* 2 (July 1933): 272-83.

———. "The Development of the Present Relationship of the Federal Government to Negro Education." *Journal of Negro Education* 7 (July 1938): 273-76.

Leavell, Ullin W. "Trends of Philanthropy in Negro Education." *Journal of Negro Education* 2 (Jan. 1933): 38-52.

Ligon, Moses A. "A History of Public Education in Kentucky." *Bulletin of the Bureau of School Service of the University of Kentucky* 14 (June 1942): 183-366.

Marshall, Thurgood. "An Evaluation of Recent Efforts to Achieve Racial Integration in Education through Resort of the Courts." *Journal of Negro Education* 21, no. 3 (summer 1952): 316-27.

Meeth, L. Richard. "The Transition of the Predominantly Negro College." *Journal of Negro Education* 35 (fall 1966): 494-505.

Miller, Kelly. "The Past, Present and Future of the Negro College. *Journal of Negro Education* 2 (July 1933): 411-15.

————. "The Reorganization of the Higher Education of the Negro in Light of Changing Conditions." *Journal of Negro Education* 5 (July 1936): 484-94.

Moon, F.D. "The Negro Public College in Kentucky and Oklahoma." *Journal of Negro Education* 31 (summer 1962): 322-29.

Murrell, Glenn. "The Desegregation of Paducah Junior College." *Register of the Kentucky Historical Society* 67 (Jan. 1969): 68-79.

Nabrit, S.M. "Desegregation and the Future of the Graduate and Professional Education in Negro Institutions." *Journal of Negro Education* 27 (summer 1958): 415.

"The Negro in Kentucky." *Negro History Bulletin* 5 (Jan. 1942): 42.

Nelson, Paul David. "Experiment in Interracial Education at Berea College, 1858-1908." *Journal of Negro History* 5 (January 1974), 13-27.

Parrish, Charles H., Jr. "Desegregation of Higher Education in Kentucky." *Journal of Negro Education* 27 (1958): 260-68.

Smith, Gerald. "Student Demonstrations and the Dilemma of the Black College President in 1960: Rufus Atwood and Kentucky State College." *Register of the Kentucky Historical Society* 88 (summer 1990): 318-34.

Smith, Harold S. "Kentucky State College and Its President." *Wilberforce University Quarterly* 2 (July 1941): 77-80.

Steele, Charles T. "Nearly 50 Years of Repeated Legal and Civic Efforts to Amend the Day Law." *Louisville Defender,* 8 July 1950.

Thomas, Herbert A. "Victims of Circumstance: Negroes in a Southern Town, 1865-1880." *Register of the Kentucky Historical Society* 71 (1973): 253-71.

Thompson, Charles H. "The Socio-Economic Status of Negro College Students." *Journal of Negro Education* 2 (Jan. 1933): 26-27.

————. "Introduction: The Problem of Negro Higher Education." *Journal of Negro Education* 2 (July 1933): 257-71.

Timberlake, Clarence L. "The Early Struggle for the Education of Blacks in the Commonwealth of Kentucky." *Register of the Kentucky Historical Society* 71 (July 1973): 225-52.

"West Kentucky Vocational School Graduates First White." *Kentucky Negro Journal* 3, no. 4 (1960): 27-28.

Wiggins, Sam P. "Dilemmas in Desegregation in Education." *Journal of Negro Education* 35 (fall 1966): 430-39.

Willie, Charles V. "Philanthropic Support and Foundation for Blacks: A Case Study from the 1960's." *Journal of Negro Education* 50 (summer 1981): 270-84.

Wilson, Atwood S. "Historical Sketch of Negro Education in Kentucky." *Kentucky School Journal* 16 (1938): 16-18.

Wright, George C. "The Founding of Lincoln Institute." *Filson Club Quarterly* 49 (Jan. 1975): 57-70.

————. "The NAACP and Residential Segregation, Louisville, Kentucky, 1914-1917." *Register of the Kentucky Historical Society* 78 (winter 1980): 35-54.

Unpublished Materials

Atwood, Rufus Ballard. "Autobiography." 1964. Typescript. R.B. Atwood Papers, Kentucky State Univ. Blazer Library Archives.

Bond, J.A. "Negro Education in Kentucky." Master's thesis, Univ. of Cincinnati, 1930.

Coleman, Lena Mae. "A History of Kentucky State College for Negroes." Master's thesis, Indiana Univ., 1938.

Collins, Ernest M. "The Political Behavior of the Negroes in Cincinnati, Ohio, and Louisville, Kentucky." Ph.D. diss., Univ. of Kentucky, 1950.

Collins, Wellyn Fitzgerald. "Louisville Municipal College: A Study of the College Founded for Negroes in Louisville, Kentucky." Master's thesis, Univ. of Louisville, 1976.

Donovan, Mary Sudman. "Kentucky Law regarding the Negro, 1865-1877." Master's thesis, Univ. of Louisville, 1967.

Edwards, Austin. "History of Kentucky State Industrial College for Negroes." Master's thesis, Indiana State Teachers College, 1936.

Engle, Frederick. "Superintendents and Issues: A Study of the Superintendents of Public Instruction of Kentucky, 1891-1943." Ed.D. diss., Univ. of Kentucky, 1966.

Fouse, William H. "An Educational History of Negroes in Lexington, Kentucky." Master's thesis, Univ. of Cincinnati, 1937.

Fraas, Elizabeth M. "Keen Johnson: Newspaperman and Governor." Ph.D. diss., Univ. of Kentucky, 1984.

Galloway, Oscar R. "Higher Education for Negroes in Kentucky." Ph.D. diss., Univ. of Kentucky, 1931.

Giles, Brooks. "A Proposed Program of Trade and Technical Area Vocational Education for Lincoln Institute, Lincoln Ridge, Shelby County, Kentucky." Master's thesis, Ohio State Univ., 1961.

Hardin, John A. "Hope versus Reality: Black Higher Education in Kentucky, 1904-1954." Ph.D. diss., University of Michigan, 1989.

Harrison, Violet. "A Study of Negro Colleges and Other Institutions Founded by the Methodist Episcopal Church." Master's thesis, Univ. of Cincinnati, 1937.

Hill, Helen Collins. "Kentucky State College: Its Transition and Future." Ph.D. diss., Southern Illinois Univ., 1971.

Hudson, James Blaine, III. "The History of Louisville Municipal College: Events Leading to the Desegregation of the University of Louisville." Ed.D. diss., Univ. of Kentucky, 1981.

Hunter, Ann Jackson Heartwell. "Against the Tide." 1983. Typescript. Photocopy in author's possession.

McElhone, Patrick Shaheen. "The Civil Rights Activities of the Louisville Branch of the NAACP." Master's thesis, Univ. of Louisville, 1976.

Meece, Leonard. "Negro Education in Kentucky." Master's thesis, Univ. of Kentucky, 1938.

Murrell, Glen. "The History of Paducah Junior College." Master's thesis, Murray State Univ., 1968.

Nichols, Claude E. "Reorganization of the Negro High Schools in Kentucky." Master's thesis, Univ. of Cincinnati, 1936.

Orr, Clyde. "An Analytical Study of the Conference of Presidents of the Negro Land Grant Colleges." Ed.D. diss., Univ. of Kentucky, 1959.

Russell, Harvey Clarence. "The Training of Teachers in the Colored Schools of Kentucky." Master's thesis, Univ. of Cincinnati, 1929.

Seals, Warren Taylor. "The Rise and Decline of Private Schools for Negroes in the State of Kentucky." Master's thesis, Univ. of Cincinnati, 1948.

Sexton, Robert R. "Kentucky Politics and Society, 1919-1932." Ph.D. diss., Univ. of Washington, 1970.

Smith, Gerald L. "Mr. Kentucky State: A Biography of Rufus Ballard Atwood." Ph.D. diss., Univ. of Kentucky, 1988.

Strother, William B. "Some Aspects of Negro Culture in Lexington, Kentucky." Master's thesis, Univ. of Kentucky, 1939.

Swafford, Juanita Chesier. "A History of Lincoln Institute High School, Lincoln Ridge, Kentucky." Master's thesis, Univ. of Louisville, 1964.

Venable, Thomas Calvin. "A History of Negro Education in Kentucky." Ed.D. diss., Peabody College for Teachers, 1952.

Williams, J.T. "A Comparative Study of the Administration of Higher Education in Selected Negro and White Colleges of Kentucky." Master's thesis, Univ. of Cincinnati, 1933.

Williams, Lawrence H. "History of Simmons University Bible College." Univ. of Louisville, 1973. Typescript.

Wright, George C. "Blacks in Louisville, 1890-1930." Ph.D. diss., Duke Univ., 1977.

Index

NAACP (National Association for the
Advancement of Colored
People): on Anderson-Mayer
Student Aid Law, 55; attacks on
segregation by, 9, 78, 98; chal-
lenges to Day Law by, 63-64,
83, 89, 91-92; effect of Johnson
case on, 97; and *Gaines* deci-
sion, 63, 75; and Kentucky
State, 157n. 10; and teacher
salaries, 71-72; weaknesses
in, 77
Nabrit, James, 93
National Association for the
Advancement of Colored People
(NAACP). *See* NAACP
natural science programs, 52
Nazareth Women's College
(Louisville), *130,* 154n. 111
"new Berea" college, 16-19, 21. *See
also* Lincoln Institute (Lincoln
Ridge)
New York Evening Post, 18
normal schools, 3, 28, 58, *124, 125*
Northern Kentucky University
(Highland Heights), 114
Norton, Eckstein, 4, 24
Nunn, Louie B., 119
nursing education, 87
Nutter, Rev. Homer, 107

Ogden, Geraldine, 108
O'Rear, Edward C., 18-19, 95
out-of-state tuition grants, 80, 96

Paducah Junior College (Paducah),
53, 96, 104-6
Parks, George, 37
Parrish, Charles Henry: as advocate
of industrial education, 24-26;
opposition to Lincoln
Independent Party by, 40; and
Simmons University, 4, 31, 32,
33-34, 43; and University of

Louisville, 40
Parrish, Dr. Charles, Jr., 102
Patterson, John, 41
Perkins, J.M., 42
Perry, William H., Jr., 19, 60, 80
Philadelphia Enquirer, 18
philosophies of education. *See* indus-
trial education; liberal arts cur-
ricula
physical education programs, 52
Pirkey, Rev. R.O., 32
Pittsburgh Courier, 55
politics: black involvement in, 54-55,
71, 83-84, 86; black leaders and,
40-41; effect of Berea case on,
18-19; and Kentucky State, 38-
39, 41, 50; and Simmons
University, 32-33
Powell, Henry Lee, 104
Prairie View Agricultural and
Mechanical College for Negroes
(Prairie View, Tx.), 91
press, black, 19-20, 78
Pruitt, Earl, 107
public affairs programs, 116

Quin, Houston, 33

Rabb, Maurice F., 80
Ransom, Leon, 78
Ray, Eloise Broady, 105
Reed, Ernest E., 29, 34
religious schools, 3
Robinson, John T., 16
Rockne, Knute, 52
Rose, Harry Eugene, 155n. 117
Rowe, John, 144n. 21
Russell, Green P., Jr., 37
Russell, Green Pinckney, 8, 36-39,
41, 42-43, 65
Russell, Harvey Clarence, 54, 56
Russell, John D., 103

Sage, Russell, 17